MEMORIES

RUSSELL L. ACKOFF

FOREWORD BY PETER SENGE

INTRODUCTION BY JOHN POURDEHNAD

ILLUSTRATIONS BY THE AUTHOR

Published in this first edition in 2010 by:
Triarchy Press
Station Offices
Axminster
Devon. EX13 5PF
United Kingdom

+44 (0)1297 631456
info@triarchypress.com
www.triarchypress.com

A catalogue record for this book is available from the British
Library.

Front cover set in *Russell Oblique*, a font designed and created by
Karen Ackoff. *Russell Oblique* is an Adobe font.

ISBN: 978-0-9565379-7-3

Contents

Contents

INTRODUCTION

Even though I had the privilege of knowing Russ Ackoff for more than thirty years, first as a PhD student at the Wharton school and later as his colleague, talking or writing about him is always a daunting task.

Ackoff used to say, "When you have a choice, you have a problem!", and the first problem with him is always, "Where to start?"

Fortunately on this occasion, Peter Senge has contributed a wonderfully generous and considered analysis of Ackoff's contribution to the world of design and systems thinking, so I can confine myself here to the man himself.

When I think about Russ, I think about the many qualities that he had. He was humble, magnanimous, ethical, honest, loyal, hard working, humorous and a true friend.

His humility when talking about his work was striking. In the years that I worked with him, I never once heard him say "I" did this or that. He was famous for his stories. Even though most of the stories were about the work that he had done for hundreds of organizations, he never once said "I" did it! It was always "we" did it. Even in these Memories, which inevitably turn the focus on him, you will find that he always uses "we" when talking about his consulting work.

He was truly generous with intellectual property and financial gains. He would always name others as coauthors, even if he had written most of the paper or book. He would never be offended if others made more money than him from a project.

One could imagine that Russ could have taken incredible financial advantage of his position as an insider with senior executives. But Russ had uncompromised ethics. A few years ago we were working for a mid size oil and gas company in the Midwest. When we started our assignment, the stock of the company was trading at $2.55. After 4 months the stock price had risen to almost $18. At the time one of the executives with the company told me privately that we should buy company stocks! I told him he obviously didn't know Ackoff! I told him that Ackoff's relationship with Anheuser Busch started in the late 1950s and continued until August Busch III retired in 2006. I told him that AB's share of the beer market in the US grew from 8% to almost 52% in that time. And I told him that Ackoff never owned even one share of the company in that time.

Another great strength of Russ's character was his loyalty to his friends. If you were fortunate enough to work with him, you would have a friend for life. Russ was always there for his friends and extended help to those who needed it. Just one example is that of the young African American community organizer Herman Wrice, who has an important place in this book. When Herman met Russ, he was a young gang leader living in the West Philadelphia neighborhood of Mantua. Russ encouraged Herman to join him in the development of a neighborhood revitalization project there during the 1970s. Herman went on to become an Ackoff collaborator for the remainder of his life. Herman's story was covered widely in the media including an episode of 60 Minutes that showed Herman and his white, hardhat collaborators working in deprived neighborhoods getting rid of drug dealers. Over the 30+ years that followed, Russ remained a financial supporter and advisor to Herman. In recent years, even after Herman had passed away, Russ returned to the Mantua community with new ideas and corporate sponsorship for neighborhood development.

Akcoff used to say that traditionally, as a result of analytical thinking, human activity is divided into three categories – work, play and learning. Being with Ackoff was truly an integration of all three. When asked by some why he worked so hard and urged to take time off and have fun, he would respond by saying: "what I do is fun for me!"

I would like to finish by touching on a characteristic that wasn't particularly obvious, unless you knew him well. His sense of humor. He and I were once at Toronto Airport waiting for our plane to Philadelphia. As usual, Russ pulled out a book and started reading it. I snuck away to the duty free shop. On my return, without looking up from his book, he said: "Where the hell were you?" I told him I had been to buy myself a men's cologne. He asked me how much I paid for it and I told him $46 ($10 less than in the US). Still without looking at me he said: "I never paid more than $2 for a cologne in my entire life." To tease him I said, "Russ you have to smell nice in case you get an opportunity to kiss a lady". Finally he turned and looked at me and said: "With a face like yours you need all the help you can get!"

Some two years before his death, Russ did me the enormous honor of bequeathing me his library and intellectual property and asking me to be his executor in that respect. It only remains for me to acknowledge the help and support I have received since that time from the many people who I came to know through Russ:

His wife Helen (Waltz) Ackoff and his daughter Karen Ackoff.

His colleagues at the Wharton School, the University of Pennsylvania and at the Ackoff Collaboratory and Ackoff Library. In particular, Larry M. Starr, Director, Organizational Dynamics Graduate Studies School of Arts and Sciences, University of Pennsylvania, for taking a lead in the establishment of the Ackoff Library and his support for the development of the Ackoff Virtual Inquiry Center (AVIC) project.

I also would like to acknowledge August Bush III for his life long support of Russ himself and of anything related to Russ (including his generous donations to the Ackoff Systems Thinking Library at the Organizational Dynamics Program, to the Ackoff Collaboratory at The Systems Engineering and to Russell Ackoff Doctoral Student Fellowships at the Wharton School, University of Pennsylvania).

Finally, I also would like to acknowledge Vince Barabba and Ray Stata for their support and generous contribution towards the creation of Ackoff Collaboratory.

John Pourdehnad
Philadelphia
July 2010

FOREWORD

Russ was an inspiration and mentor to many of us, as one of the true pioneers of the systems perspective in management. He probably understood the systems perspective in its historical evolution as well or better than anyone, and saw this age as the one where many forces might converge in helping to shift the tragically reductionistic and fragmented thinking that dominates modern institutions, from business to government to schools.

I entered the systems field from engineering and then the engineering-oriented system dynamics approach at MIT with its emphasis on better models and modeling. The premise underlying this approach was that so long as people think in fragmented ways they will act similarly. The emphasis was on helping managers develop better policies based on explicit analysis of the consequences of existing policies seen from a larger systemic perspective. While this approach was radical methodologically, it tended to be conservative institutionally. The initial premise was that those in senior positions had the vested interest to act in accord with the longer term well being of the institution and would, with proper guidance from the system dynamics analysts, do so. Russ had, I think, a more realistic view of the deep structural flaws with the modern corporation that made it unlikely that many 'philosopher kings' would manage to overcome the relentless pressures for choosing short term benefit over longer term health. (Later, Jay Forrester, the founder of system dynamics, came to a similar view and their thinking converged on the need for radical redesign of the corporation itself – but this view remained more an add-on to the methodological orientation of system dynamics; many people are working today in the continued effort to integrate the two in my judgment.)

For me Russ was an incisive, lifelong critic of the modern organizational form. He saw its limitations and argued for radical redesign. He was an advocate for major re-visioning and processes of change that started with helping people see what they truly valued and where they truly wanted to get – and then working backwards to see what it would take to get there. Anything less would simply lead to naive incrementalism, where 90% of what had been would be preserved while people tinkered around the edges with change that would never amount to "too much change". Russ was not worried about too much change.

I think Russ gave us all courage to be bold, while also appreciating that the overall undertaking is still in its infancy. The inherited traditions over generations toward patriarchy, authoritarian views of leadership, and rigid systems of institutional power will not change in a generation. The physicist David Bohm believed that the root source of our deepest problems stemmed from "fragmentation" of thought, which he felt had its origins in the agricultural revolution and the perceived separation of human and nature. Obviously the "systems revolution" that Russ foresaw and helped to launch will unfold over generations not years. How long will it take before we can give up the cultural myth of domination over nature, that nature exists to serve our needs? How long before we shed the perceptual habit of objectification, "seeing" the other as a separate object as opposed to a distinct being that inter-depends with our own being? How long will we preserve the belief that power comes from institutional position versus connection to the creative flow of the universe? It is easy to feel daunted by such questions – but I think that too comes from a shallow appreciation of the systems perspective. The forces for change come from "life's longing for itself", not from ego-based human striving. I believe Russ sensed this and for this reason encouraged us all to simply do what we can, knowing that there is a much large river into which our efforts flow.

Peter Senge
MIT and SoL
July 2010

PREFACE

The past is normally treated as a continuous flow of events embedded in time. But this, of course, is not the way we remember it. We remember it as a series of discrete happenings and even then not necessarily in the order in which they occurred. This memoir consists of a set of discrete bits and pieces of the past. They are what stand out in my memory and hopefully are something that readers might find useful and, if not useful, entertaining.

Please keep in mind that an author's memories of things past (like any other human's memories) are reconstructions: the way s/he would like them to have happened, not necessarily how they did happen. An author is seldom aware of the distortions s/he has imposed on the past. The criterion I used was to select incidents from which I thought I had learned something useful. I have tried to indicate what was learned from each incident.

In general, the incidents described here are of a type not covered in textbooks or university courses. In general, incidents covered in textbooks have been dehumanized. But it is precisely the humanity in them that is their most valuable aspect. The deletion of this human aspect from a story makes the teller more like a robot than a person.

Life is a series of relationships formed and dissolved, with a few exceptions. Those relationships that persist do so because of continual communication between the parties involved. Any reflective academic who does consulting "on the side" knows that, unless s/he is seen as a friend of the one receiving his/her advice, it is unlikely to be accepted and acted on. The relationship that develops between a consultant and the one served is the strongest variable affecting the predictability and consequences of their relationship.

Those who have attended one or more of my lectures will be aware
of the fact that I make liberal use of stories based on my experience.
I have found, when coming into contact with people who have
"heard" me, that they remember the stories much better than
the point they were used to illustrate. They remember the stories
precisely because they are humanized and not abstract. The stories
also capture the principal source of satisfaction I derive from doing
what I do.

I hope this particular set of stories will enable the reader to share
in the pleasure the events brought and still bring to me in their
retelling.

Russ Ackoff

Memories

Philippines: Rice Paddies

As an enlisted man in the Second World War, I was working on preparing the engineering plan for the invasion of the Philippines. This was being done in a camp site in northern New Guinea. The overall plan of the invasion was prepared under the direction of General Seibert, head of the X Corps, of which our section was a part. When I received a copy of his plan, I was alarmed. He planned to beach a good deal of armored equipment on the first day of the invasion. We checked our aerial photographs of the location of the landing and they showed extensive rice paddies between the beach on which we were to land and the one paved road on the island. This road ran parallel to the beach a short distance inland. Armored equipment would not be able to reach the road by going through the rice paddies unless a road was first built across the paddies.

I showed the photographs to the Colonel who headed the engineering section of the Corps' headquarters. He was alarmed. Together we went to see the General to describe our finding. The General rejected our information saying that he had first hand intelligence from natives of the island who had recently been brought off it by submarine.

The Colonel ordered another flight over the beach on which the invasion was to begin and a new set of photographs of it. When they arrived we were able to assert with certainty that there were rice paddies where we had said they were. Back we went to the General. He insisted once again that his information was superior to ours. The Colonel then told the General that he would not accept any responsibility for the planned landing. In anger, the General relieved the Colonel of his post there and then, and later assigned him to another unit.

We landed on the east coast of Leyte in September of 1944 and the rice paddies were there. The beach was quickly covered with immobilized armored equipment. Our air cover, which was provided by the Navy from off shore, was unexpectedly called away to engage with the Japanese navy in the Battle of Leyte, one of the most decisive in the war. Left without cover we were bombed from a very low altitude by Japanese airplanes. Much of the equipment was destroyed in the first few days of the invasion.

LESSON LEARNED:

The mouth of an informer should not outrank the eyes of the beholder.

WORLD WAR II: SLIT TRENCHES

In planning the invasion of the Philippines each section of the X Corps headquarters was instructed to have its commanding officer and two enlisted men be part of the landing party. I was selected as one of the enlisted men. The Lieutenant Colonel who headed our engineering section was replaced by a Captain who was under his command. We received no explanation of the substitution.

We left New Guinea for the Philippines on LSTs, troop-carrying landing craft. It was terribly hot at sea. As a result we spent most of the time sitting on deck trying to capture the slight breeze. One day when sitting next to the Master Sergeant who served the commanding general, I referred to the substitution of the Captain for the Lieutenant Colonel. The Sergeant explained. He said the Colonel had asked General Seibert to replace him with the Captain, not a member of the regular army, because the Captain would have no other chance to participate in a landing and he wanted to do so. On the other hand, he, a regular Army officer, would have many such chances. The General responded favorably.

We asked the Captain if this were the case. He denied ever having asked for such a change. We concluded the Colonel was a coward. He was far from popular even before this revelation.

Because of almost continuous bombardment from above by Japanese aircraft, we spent several nights in slit trenches. A few nights after the landing I was awakened in my slit trench by a messenger and told that the Colonel had just landed and wanted me to dig a slit trench for him. I refused.

The messenger disappeared but later returned and told me I would be court-martialed if I did not appear to dig that trench. Again I refused. I was confident that I could avert a court martial by telling the Colonel I would reveal his duplicity. I would let him know this in the morning.

Early the next morning before he could initiate a court martial, the Colonel left by Jeep for a meeting with General MacArthur who had also landed the day before. On the way to the meeting the Colonel's Jeep came under attack from the air; he and his driver were seriously wounded.

He was rescued by the medics and shortly thereafter returned to the States. There was no court martial.

LESSON LEARNED:
Being right is not nearly as important as being lucky.

Leyte: The Morgue

Moving from east to west on the island of Leyte in the Philippines during the war, we came to the small village of Carigara. Just as we arrived the Japanese began to bomb us from the air. We had not had time to dig slit trenches but, fortunately, we saw a concrete building nearby that had been built for the Philippine army. We entered it. It was pitch black inside, had no windows and the electricity had been interrupted by the bombing. Feeling our way around we found what appeared to our touch to be a room full of cots. Some were occupied. We stretched out on ones that were not.

Quite a while later the lights came back on. One of our group woke up and started screaming. On awakening he had looked around and seen a number of dead soldiers lying on cots. The room served as a morgue. The soldier thought he was dead and screamed in terror.

We called medics. He was taken away and cared for. He was eventually sent back to the States.

Lesson Learned:
There is nothing more life-threatening than waking up dead.

Philippines and the Nature of Development

During the Second World War I landed on the island of Leyte in the Philippines in the first wave. I was a sergeant at the time, attached to the Engineering Section of the Tenth Corps Headquarters. My assignment involved engineering reconnaissance – traveling with the First Cavalry Division in order to locate construction materials that could be used to build roads, runways, aircraft shelters, and so on.

Very near the end of hostilities I was on the west coast of the island about as far from Headquarters as one could get when I received a message. It instructed me to return to Headquarters at once and report to the commanding officer, General Seibert.

The only reason I could think of to explain the call was that I had been found to be insubordinate again. I arrived late at night back at Headquarters on the east coast near the only town of consequence, Tacloban. The next morning I dressed appropriately and reported to the General. After a short delay I was shown into his office. He was seated behind a large desk. He greeted me and instructed me to be at ease and sit down in a chair in front of his desk. He did not look angry. This was a relief and my apprehension dissipated. He was fingering through a large file on his desk.

He apparently found what he was looking for, turned and addressed me. "You were trained as an architect before you were inducted into the Army, right?" I nodded agreement. He asked where I had received my training. I told him at the University of Pennsylvania. He wanted to know if and when I had completed my degree. I told him I had received my degree in May of 1941, about half a year before Pearl Harbor and my induction into the army. He asked if I had ever worked in an architect's office. I told him that I had. He wanted to know when. I told him for several summers before graduation from Penn and upon graduation. He asked what type of work the architectural firm had done. I described the largely commercial architecture in which it was engaged. Then he closed the file he had been consulting and said: "I think you will do."

He then told me that the invasion of Leyte was almost over and would be finished in a very short while. I knew this. He then said the troops were tired and needed some rest and recreation. He wanted to build a recreation center at a site he had selected. It was to accommodate several hundred soldiers for about three days at a time. He said he would like me to undertake its design and construction. He asked if I would I be willing to do so. He could have ordered me to do so but it wasn't necessary; it was like being invited to heaven after a sojourn in hell.

He asked me to join him on a small craft, a Landing Craft Infantry (LCI), for a trip to the site he had selected. We went north and rounded the tip of the island and continued about a mile south until we came to large clearing on the west bank of the river. It was a level field bordered by the river and thick woods. We disembarked and walked over the site. He asked if I thought it was suitable. I said it was great. Among other things we would be able to have activities on the water. We reboarded the boat and started back to the Headquarters.

On the return journey I asked how many engineers he was going to provide me with. He looked at me with surprise and said he could not afford to put any engineers on the job. Then I asked how I was expected to build it. He told me he would provide enough money for me to hire 150 natives to help in the construction. I told him I could not speak their language. He said he would provide an interpreter. "What about security?" I asked.

There was still sniping on the island. He said he would also supply several military police. "What materials will be made available to me?" I asked. He said: "None. Use whatever the natives use to build their shacks." These shacks were built using only three natural materials: the trunks of coconut trees for the stilts on which they rested, bamboo of which the main structure was built, and nipa, a long grass that was used to make a type of shingle over a bamboo strip. I explained that in my training as an architect I had not been taught how to use these materials. He said: "Well, learn how." I gulped at all this but was unwilling to allow the opportunity to slip through my fingers however impossible it seemed to me.

The next day, armed with an interpreter, I went to a small village very near the site the General had selected to examine the structures the natives had built. They were very primitive shacks set on stilts to avoid the washes and flooding caused by the rain during the monsoons. The cottages were about 10 feet by 12 feet and limited by the length of the bamboo they could get to span the exterior walls. I made some inquiries using my interpreter and identified those whom the villagers thought were their best builders. Two brothers were named. I found them and asked if they would build a "house" for me. I would pay them, of course. They asked me why I wanted a house since the tent city in which headquarters was located offered a higher quality of life than their village. I explained that I did not want the shack to live in but wanted to see how they built it. I told them they could have the "house" when it was completed. They could not resist and agreed to build a shack for me.

I spent the next week with them as they gathered the materials required to build the shack and then built it. When this was completed I returned to headquarters to design the facility. I planned a large recreation hall, outdoor fields for playing a variety of games, and swimming facilities. In addition, there would be showers but no dormitories. Those attending the facility would have to sleep in tents on cots that would be provided.

Before I could start construction there were several material problems I had to solve. First, I noted that all their shacks leaned slightly in the direction of the prevailing wind. When I inquired they told me they made the joints by tying two pieces of bamboo together using long blades of grass. When moist, these joints tended to loosen. This made the shack give a little in a strong wind. I wanted stiff joints. Fortunately, I could use abandoned Signal Corps wire left around the island. With a little experimentation I figured out how to use it to make an inflexible joint.

I wanted to build a dock that would go out far enough in the river at low tide to reach a sufficient depth for swimming. This required a dock about fifty feet long. The dock would have to hold about fifty men at a time. The only thing long enough, the trunks of coconut trees, would not float. Instead, using bamboo I built a bamboo cage, the bottom of which was open. It was filled with empty and sealed fifty-five gallon drums that were also plentiful around the island. They had been used to bring fuel ashore. The drums, with holes punched in their bottoms, were also to be used to make showers.

When these two problems were solved I returned to the site and hired 100 men to gather the materials and do the construction, and 50 women to weave the "shingles" out of nipa draped over bamboo. These would be used as wall and roof coverings. When the exterior walls of the recreation hall were put up the men began to gesticulate wildly at me, telling me that I would not be able to put a roof on because no bamboo was long enough to span even the lesser dimension, about 40 feet. I kept telling them not to worry but they continued to issue warnings. Then one day they saw me build a truss out of bamboo, one that was long enough to span the walls and hold the roof. They had never seen a truss before.

They were also amazed when we launched the dock and anchored it on two posts made out of the trunks of coconut palm trees on which the dock could rise and fall with the tide. One day while I was in the river, nude, working on anchoring the dock to the poles, the General appeared in his boat. I did not see him coming. When I did, I jumped up on the dock and saluted him. He broke out laughing and told me he had never been saluted before by a nude soldier.

Eventually the facility was completed. We had a modest ceremony for its opening. The entire village joined the military personnel in the celebration. When the ceremony was over the villagers returned to their homes. In the next week, using what they had learned in building the recreation facility, many of them built new shacks that were considerably larger and contained more conveniences than the old ones had.

Lesson Learned:
Development is not a matter of how much one has but of how much one can do with whatever one has.

PhD: Language Exams

In the 1940s one was required to pass two foreign language examinations in order to receive a PhD at the University of Pennsylvania. I chose to take French and German. I anticipated no problem with French because I had studied the language both in high school and during undergraduate work in architecture. I had had no exposure to German. I anticipated problems here.

I was to take the examinations in the fall of 1947. That summer my thesis supervisor and friend, C. West Churchman, and I were using the Cornel University library in Ithaca, New York. We were working on our book, *Methods of Inquiry*. Although I anticipated no problem with French I went to the library and took the first book I saw on philosophy in French. It was a book by Renan whose title was *L'Avenir de La Science,* (The Future of Science). I picked up the book off and on during the summer and read part of it using a French-English dictionary to refresh my French vocabulary.

German was another matter. I had to start from ground zero. I bought a book called *Minimum German* by Schreibner and Saline. I tried to memorize the basics but found it intolerable. I hated it. Finally, about midsummer, I said to myself, "The hell with it". I would rely on the use of a dictionary during the examination. One was allowed to do so for one's minor language, German in my case, but not on one's major language, French in my case. Churchman was very worried about my decision. He called Bob Reuman who was one of my classmates in graduate philosophy and asked him to join us in Ithaca and tutor me in German. Bob had been raised in a family where German was commonly spoken and he was fluent in the language.

He joined us and undertook the tutelage. My resistance to learning the language discouraged and infuriated him. Eventually he gave up in disgust. I decided I would do what I could from a position of almost compete ignorance of the language. I expected to fail and not get the PhD because of this deficiency.

In September I appeared for the first examination in French. To my amazement the passage given to me to translate was one from the Renan book, which I had used to brush up with. Therefore, this examination was "a breeze".

Shortly thereafter Bob Reuman and I appeared for the German examination. We were given a passage from Hegel's *Philosophy of Right*. It has been said of Hegel that he should have been translated from whatever language he used into German. His German was difficult even for those fluent in the language. I used my dictionary for most words but finished with absolute gobbledygook. It was apparent that I would never pass the examination with my alleged translation.

Fortunately, I had had a course on Hegel and thought I understood what he was trying to convey in the passage. I threw away my examination book and got a fresh one. I wrote in my English what I thought the passage was saying. Bob Reuman, of course, tackled the passage literally and had no particular problem with it.

The results of both examinations were posted a short time later. I passed the French as expected. However, much to my surprise I passed the German examination but Bob had not. What kind of justice was that? Bob took the exam the next time around and passed it then. I doubt that he ever forgave me.

LESSON LEARNED:

The only thing that can replace knowledge of another language is luck.

Warner-Swasey: Immunity to Bad Forecasts

One of the earliest industrial projects I worked on involved the Warner and Swasey Company in Cleveland, Ohio. At the time, the early 1950s, I was on the faculty of Case Institute of Technology where C. West Churchman and I had established an Operations Research Group. The Company was a major producer of turret lathes. Demand for such lathes was erratic and very difficult, if not impossible, to forecast satisfactorily. Large fluctuations occurred from month to month and year to year. The machines were very expensive and, as a result, so was an inventory of them. In addition, they took a long time to produce and, therefore, could not be produced to order quickly enough to satisfy customers. We could find no way of obtaining a satisfactory forecast, but we saw a possible alternative.

Was there another product that required the same technology and materials to make and that had a counter cyclical demand? We thought there was and we found one: mobile road-building equipment. Turret lathe sales tended to go up when economic times were good but road building equipment sales tended to go up when economic times were bad. We identified a company that made such equipment, Gradall, and Warner-Swasey acquired it. They experienced the benefits we predicted from doing so.

Lesson Learned:

Counter-cyclical products immunize against bad forecasts. For every nipple for a baby's bottle there is a condom that opposes it.

Case Institute: Security Clearance

I joined Case Institute of Technology in September 1951 as a Research Associate. I was employed to work on an Air Force project (Doan Brook) directed at producing a defensive weapon. The contract required Case to provide an Operations Research (OR) group for inputs to the development process. I was employed to head that very small group. It required a security clearance. Like the others on the project I received a temporary clearance before joining the project.

About a year later, all temporary clearances involved on the project were reviewed by I know not whom. I was denied permanent clearance and therefore had to withdraw from the project. I joined West Churchman in developing an academic program and research group in Operations Research with the Engineering Administration Department. The degree program we established was the first of its type in the United States. Case became a mecca for Operations Researchers living in, or visiting, the United States.

I decided to challenge the government's decision to deny me clearance. President Eisenhower had recently established the Industrial Review Board for this purpose. My appeal went to this Board. Fortunately, Keith Glennan, Case's president, and Clay Hollister, my departmental chairman, approved of my appeal and assured me of their support. My colleague and very close friend, Tom Cowan, who was in the Law School at Wayne University in Detroit, which I had just left, agreed to serve as my counsel. He had been one of my professors at Penn and had become a very close friend before I left that institution.

Our first effort was to find out what were the charges leveled against me. All we could get out of the Board was that there were seventeen, but not their content. We appealed to Senator Bricker, from Ohio, and he augmented our effort to learn what the charges were. Only about five were released. They included charges of guilt by association, teaching radical doctrines in my classes and publishing radical articles in an academic journal.

Guessing as well as we might the nature of the other charges, Tom and I prepared as many relevant depositions as we could. They involved student and faculty members, current and past, and university administrators. The only refusals to prepare such depositions came from nationally prominent liberal philosophers. They were concerned about being charged with guilt by association with me.

The three-day hearing was held in Washington, DC. before a five-man Board. The chairman sat one end of the table; I sat at the other end with Tom Cowan on my right. Witnesses we called sat on my left. It was a grueling three days. I had to engage in a number of heated arguments to the effect that, although my thinking was radical, I had never supported a revolution. My efforts were to make the country better, not to overthrow its government. For example, I was asked by the Army Colonel on the Board if I believed in God. I said I could not answer until he told me what concept of God he was referring to. He charged me with evading the question. I replied by saying that I had studied each of the major religions of the world and had attended services in the places of worship of those that permitted it. I found the concepts of God held by each religion differed significantly from each other.

He continued his charge of evasion. I asked him if by God he meant an old man with a long beard sitting on a throne up in heaven, surrounded by little nude angels flying about. He said not. I pressed for his concept. He continued to evade while charging me with doing so. The chairman broke in saying that unless the

Colonel was willing to answer my question I could not answer his. That ended the discussion.

One charge was that my course on modern philosophy covered the work of Karl Marx. I said that was true. It also covered the work of Thomas Jefferson, Tom Payne and Abraham Lincoln. I read some carefully selected passages from their works without revealing their source and asked if these were statements they considered to be disloyal to the United States. They said a number of them were. I then revealed their sources. I argued that a diversity of opinion went to make up our country and that we had an obligation to let our students know that diversity. I argued that it was in the diversity of opinion in our country that the principal source of its strength lay, not in conformity to an official set of opinions.

The "guilt by association" charge involved having an article published in a philosophy journal whose editor was a "fellow traveler". I told the Board I had no idea as to the political beliefs of the editor because the nature of our interaction did not involve such knowledge. I admitted to frequent arguments, sometimes in public, with representatives of different leftist groups. They told me that I was charged with belonging to each of them. I pointed out the contradiction in the beliefs of these groups, all of which were represented on campus, and that one could not belong to all simultaneously. And on and on it went.

When the hearing was adjourned at the end of the third day I was told I would receive their verdict within two weeks. I asked for a transcript of the sessions to which I was entitled according to the charter of the Board. As we were leaving the room, the chairman told me privately that he appreciated the education he had received in the last few days. I was greatly encouraged by this.

Two weeks later I was notified that I had been granted permanent clearance. Immediately on receiving this notice, I resigned from the Air Force project and said I would never work on classified material again, and I never have. I did not receive a transcript and after numerous efforts to get one, because I wanted to publish it, I was told the transcript had been lost. I never believed it. I am sure it was the result of the Board or some other authority not wishing to let the proceedings become public. It would have discredited the process.

I moved on to the faculty of the Engineering Administration Department and remained there until 1964 when I left to join The Wharton School of the University of Pennsylvania.

LESSON LEARNED:

Security clearance is a way of stopping an epidemic: the spreading of ideas.

India and the USA's Foreign Aid

In 1957 I was invited to India by Professor P. C. Mahalanobis to provide a critique of the five-year plan that had been prepared under his direction. My wife was included in the invitation. A major portion of my time in India was spent at his Indian Statistical Institute in its guest house. Mahalanobis and his wife Rani were a wonderful host and hostess. They went to a great deal of trouble to keep me and my wife occupied and exposed to Indian culture. A number of receptions were held at the Institute to which prominent Americans visiting India at that time were invited. The Ford Foundation was more than adequately represented at these functions.

I was repeatedly subjected to Ford's disappointment with India's response to its efforts to introduce family planning. At one such gathering a Vice President of the Ford Foundation pointed out to me that although the Indian economy was growing rapidly, its population was growing more rapidly. As a result, average income and purchasing power were declining. He cited this as evidence of India's irrationality.

By this time I had been saturated with the whining of Ford's representatives. I suggested to the Vice President the possibility that it was Ford that was irrational and not the Indians. He challenged me to produce any evidence to this effect. By chance I was carrying a clipping from the English language newspaper that cited a Brazilian woman who had just had her 32nd child. I pointed out that, even if we took this as abnormal, we might consider twenty children as the number a woman could have during her reproductive life. If the average Indian woman had six children in her life, I was more impressed by the approximately 14 she did not have than by the approximately six she did have. I argued that, therefore, the large – by American standards – size of Indian families was not due to lack of birth control. The Vice President dismissed my argument with disgust and moved away from me.

Another guest, P. K. Balakrishnan, then came up to me and introduced himself as the head of the Demography Department of the Institute. He apologized for having listened to my exchange with the Ford representative. Then he said he thought my argument was a telling one. He would like to conduct related research and asked if I would work with him on it.

Because my visit was soon to end I suggested that my replacement, my colleague at Case, Glen Camp, work with him. I was sure Glen would be anxious to do so. Arrangements for this collaboration were completed before I left India.

Balakrishnan and Camp noted that India had no form of social security and no unemployment insurance. Nevertheless, average life expectancy had significantly increased since India had gained its independence. But because young people were constantly being fed into the workforce, years of unemployment faced most men, beginning in their middle age. The only kind of security available to them was private support from others. Sons were the most likely source of such support. Balakrishnan and Camp calculated how many sons would be required to support two unemployed adults who, on average, would have an equal number of girls who were then unemployable. (Girls were not an asset but a liability since their marriage would require a dowry.) Balakrishnan and Camp took into account infant and childhood mortality. It turned out that the average Indian family was exactly the size required to support two unemployed adults.

They checked these results by comparing families that had three sons in a row with those that had three daughters. Those with three sons normally stopped having children without the benefit of aid from the Ford Foundation. Those with three daughters were just getting started.

Lesson Learned:

Where there is no social security, wage-earning children are the next best thing, but they require a long-term investment and reciprocating affection.

India: On the Generosity of the Poor

My wife and I fell in love with India's classical music and dance. I was particularly taken with Indian drums (tablas). My wife decided to surprise me and buy a pair. She inquired from the concierge at our hotel where she could make such a purchase. She then took a taxi, driven by a Sikh, as most were, to the store where she bought the tablas. She had the driver wait for her while she made the purchase.

When she came out of the store carrying the drums, the driver, Kirpal Singh, through gesture and stumbling English, made it clear that he played the tablas. He volunteered to come to the hotel in the evening when I had returned from work and show me how to use them. My wife accepted the offer.

That evening Kirpal and I had a great time, he on the drums, me on my harmonica. Shortly after we had begun there was a knock at our door. I opened it to find the hotel manager, who expressed concern over our having been invaded by a low-caste Sikh. We explained that he was with us by invitation. The manager left but with a skeptical expression on his face.

From then on for the rest of the week we were in Calcutta, Kirpal waited at the entrance to the hotel for my wife. He would take no other customers. He became a dedicated guide for her and me, when I was available. We spent evenings together and on a weekend he took us to his temple where New Year was being celebrated. We were given places on the dais for the ceremony. He took us to the Taj Mahal and Fatehpur Sikri, two of the most beautiful structures in India. The Taj exceeded even our bloated expectations.

On the day we were packing to leave Kirpal came up to our hotel room. I offered to give him anything I had. He was very reluctant to accept anything but eventually accepted one sweater.

We were to be taken to the airport by the Institute's limousine. Kirpal objected and insisted we go with him in his cab. He cried when I explained that we had to accept the Institute's hospitality. I then changed the arrangements. My wife went to the airport in the Institute's limousine and I went with Kirpal in his cab. At no time during the week would he accept payment from us. Just before we left our hotel room for the airport he brought his brother to our room because he could speak some English. He asked us if we had enough money to get home because, if not, Kirpal wanted to give us some. It took some convincing to persuade him that we had no need for additional funds.

I never became any good on the drums but they were a constant reminder of one of the most remarkable and generous men I had ever met. He has been on my mind for more than fifty years.

LESSON LEARNED:
The worth of a man is not how much he has but how much of what he has he is willing to give to others.

India Could Not Be Buttered Up

While I was in India in 1957 the US Government announced that it was going to dry dock the merchant marine fleet that had been used in World War II to supply our troops. The Indian Government offered to buy the ships. The US was reluctant to sell them to India because it believed that the Indians would use them for international shipping. This it believed would unsettle that transportation business significantly. India assured the US it would use the vessels only for intracoastal shipping. Apparently the US government did not trust the Indian Government and it said no. However, our government apparently felt some guilt and offered to sell India our surplus butter at a bargain price.

India, of course, did not use butter; it used ghee. Moreover it had no refrigeration with which to keep butter fresh. The Indians laughed at the offer and pointed out to me what they took to be a major characteristic of American aid. The aid was offered to solve an American problem – in this case a surplus of butter – and not an Indian problem.

Lesson Learned:
In the United States, foreign aid is domestic aid in disguise.

England: The University of Birmingham

I spent the academic year 1959-1960 in England at the University of Birmingham.

I had received no orientation on the University's culture. As a result I committed a number of booboos. There were two that did not endear me to the Chairman of the Department I joined. He had arranged a luxurious office for me next to his own. I declined and instead took a very small room in a temporary building built during World War II. The Operations Research (OR) Group was housed in that building and I wanted to be with them. This, I discovered, was insulting to the Chairman.

In a Departmental meeting at which the Chairman introduced me to the faculty he had asked me to make some remarks. After his laudatory introduction I thanked him, addressing him by his first name. Another booboo; I had no right to assume a familiarity that justified use of his first name.

I found that the small group working in my field was not engaged in any projects directed at solving real problems in real organizations, as my group in the States was heavily engaged in. When I inquired about this I was told that University regulations precluded work with a profit-making organization. It would be prostitution of an academic pursuit. Curiously, my presence there was made possible by a visiting chair endowed by the Joseph Lucas Corporation, the largest producer of automotive parts in the UK. During my initial meeting with my benefactors, I expressed surprise at this to one of the executives in the company. He told me that in the past he had tried to contract the OR group in the University for some work for his company but had been rebuffed each time. Then, working together we decided to ignore this constraint and see what would happen.

Pretending to be unaware of the alleged University regulation we drew up a contract for work to be done by the OR group. I submitted the contract to the University's financial officer. He processed it without any word back to me about the alleged regulation. After we got the work under way, we arranged several other contracts with corporations with no difficulty. It turned out that the faculty member's belief in a constraining regulation was a self-fulfilling prophesy and was completely wrong.

Shortly after arriving in England I went to Holland to deliver a lecture at a university there. I left my family back in Birmingham because the trip was very short. It was my first trip outside the UK. When I returned I was stopped by an immigration officer at the airport. It turned out that I had not read about a requirement that I register with a local police station once I was settled in England. For this reason they said I could not re-enter England and would have to fly back to the United States. I did not protest but asked them to arrange two things. First, to let the University know about this so they could arrange a substitute for me in the classes and research projects for which I was responsible. Second, to arrange for my family – wife and three children two of whom were in school in Birmingham – to be returned to the States. When they heard these two requests they asked me to wait while they consulted a higher authority.

They were gone a while. When they returned they told me I could return to Birmingham but that I had to register at a police station by the day after my return. If I failed to do so I would be deported. I complied.

LESSON LEARNED:
Ignorance of customs is even more costly than ignorance of the law.

Holland: Diapers in Dutch

After my sabbatical year in England (1960-1961) at the University of Birmingham, my family and I went to Denmark to spend some time with friends and vacation for a while. After a great few weeks there we packed our three children into our Volkswagen Beetle and drove to Bilthoven in Holland. On the way we ran into a good deal of stop-and-go driving. We came to one of our many stops behind a large truck. We were flanked on both sides by other trucks. This stop seemed to be inordinately long. My eight-year-old son suddenly said, "Hey, we're moving". The car was not moving but the road appeared to be. We got out of the car and moved to the side of the "road" only to find we had driven onto a ferry and were on our way to Amsterdam.

When we arrived in Amsterdam we looked for a drug store with some urgency. We had run out of disposable diapers for Karla, our youngest. After a few inquiries, we found one. My wife and I went in. In Denmark we had learned that the brand name for the diapers we wanted was "Sanex". We asked the pharmacist for Sanex. He nodded and disappeared into the back of the store. He reappeared with a small package wrapped in brown paper with no brand or product designation on it. The package was much too small for diapers. We indicated this by sign language and by repeating, "Too small, too small".

The pharmacist indicated that he understood and disappeared once again. He returned with a package exactly like the first except it was a bit larger. But it too was not large enough to contain diapers. We went through the "too small" ritual again. He nodded to indicate that he understood and returned to the back of the store. He reappeared with a package much like the previous ones but a little larger. However, it was still not large enough. We went into our act again but the pharmacist told us by sign language and repeating some words in Dutch that this last one was the largest available.

Now we knew we were getting the wrong product. I removed a handkerchief from my pants pocket and proceeded to fold it on the counter as one would a diaper. He lit up. He got it. He disappeared and returned this time with a package of Sanex diapers clearly so indicated on the package.

We were curious as to what was contained in the first three packages. He eventually understood and he let me and my tiny wife know that they contained sanitary napkins.

LESSON LEARNED:

Brand names are not always product names; those that are, like Xerox or Jello, are the lucky ones.

AIR FORCE INVENTORY

The Case OR (Operations Research) Group received a contract from the Air Force to determine how best to manage the maintenance and repair of aircraft in the field during combat. A very large inventory of spare parts was required. This inventory was difficult to move around with a mobile Air Force.

Early in the study we found that the cost of one each of every part of a combat airplane exceeded the cost of an assembled airplane by a large amount. As a result, we suggested that no inventory of spare parts be carried and moved about, but that extra airplanes be purchased. Then spare parts could be removed (cannibalized) from the last airplane waiting for work to be done on it. It would also be easy to identify the part needed and complex numeric identification would not be required. Planes can be moved from a maintenance and repair facility in the same way they were originally brought to that repair facility. The time required to put a plane or its replacement back into service is significantly reduced in this system.

LESSON LEARNED:

The sum of the costs of the parts may be greater than the cost of the whole.

Air Force Noise

The Air Force contracted with the research group at Case (of which I was a part) to determine how to improve communication between two parties when an intelligent third party was trying to obstruct it. For example, in combat, enemies try to jam communication between ground and aircraft in flight. The enemy is assumed to have equipment that can detect the frequency of a transmission very quickly. Therefore, when ground starts a communication the enemy can quickly make it unreadable by jamming the frequency used. If ground changes frequency because of jamming, the enemy can detect this quickly and jam the new frequency. Even though ground can change the channel it uses very quickly, the enemy can detect this and effectively block communication to a pilot in the air.

One cannot get around this difficulty by using coded messages because they too can be jammed by an intelligent enemy.

While working on this problem the team members consulted Marshall McLuhan's writing to the effect that the medium is the message. This suggested that the frequency of a transmission be used as a symbol rather than a symbol transmitted over that frequency. In this way, changes of frequency could be used to deliver a message and jamming would have no effect.

Lesson Learned:
The frequency of a message may reveal more than its content.

Army: Vehicle Maintenance

At Case Institute of Technology we obtained a contract with the US Army's Transportation Department. We were asked to see if longer life and greater up-time could be obtained for 2½ ton trucks, helicopters and Jeeps. It was an unclassified project.

Since all three vehicles were also available for civilian use, we focused on comparisons between their military and civilian use. For example, the Post Office used the same Jeep as the Army. In all three cases we found civilian users got longer life and more up-time despite using less preventive maintenance. In fact we found that preventive maintenance in the Army was the principal reason for excess downtime and shorter life. Steam cleaning of vehicles after each use was a major cause of this.

We submitted our report, with recommendations and supporting data, to the contracting agency. The Army had the right to go over it and request some rewriting, which we were free to accept or not. The report was perceived by the contracting agency as threatening to the Army. It felt that if Congress got hold of the report it would reduce the equipment budget. So it classified the report as secret and thus kept it out of Congress's hands. They returned it to us with their suggested modifications. But it came to us as a classified document and we were not cleared for it. We returned the material unopened and heard no more about it.

Lesson Learned:
Security classification is a more a way of denying access to internal enemies than to external ones.

ARMY: SECURING TALK

In the 1960s I was invited to address a conference of senior Army officers to be held in the Research Triangle in North Carolina. I accepted. Shortly thereafter I received a number of forms required for obtaining clearance. I called the officer who had invited me to speak and told him my talk would not contain classified material. He told me that the meeting itself was classified and that I would not be allowed in the meeting room without the proper clearance. I told him I would not apply for clearance; if the Army required it, let the Army request it. He told me this was not possible. The invitation to speak was withdrawn.

A short time later I received a communication saying that I had been cleared and given the equivalent rank of a Brigadier General. I was invited back to the meeting but told that I could not attend any of it except my own presentation.

I arrived at the meeting room just as I was being introduced and left immediately on conclusion of my remarks.

LESSON LEARNED:
Security clearance has more to do with limiting access to information than protecting security.

Behr-Manning: Fee Association

Shortly after I joined Case Institute of Technology in Cleveland, Ohio, in 1961 I was invited to give a talk to a group of managers drawn from a wide variety of corporations. After the lecture, my first to a group of corporate managers, I was approached by a vice president of the Behr-Manning Corporation. He asked if I would be willing to give a talk to the management of his company. I said I would. He asked what my fee would be. Although I had never given a talk to a group from the private sector, I had given some presentations to the government. As an Associate Professor I was entitled to, and therefore charged, $35 per day. I quoted him the same amount for a presentation to his company. He left me with word that he would "be in touch".

I did not hear from that vice president until, about a year later, I ran into him again. I could not resist asking why I had not heard from him after our last meeting. He said his management thought that anyone who would speak to them for $35 per day could not be worth much. I asked what would have been appropriate. He said $200 per day. I told him that was my fee from then on.

A short while later I received an invitation to address the company's management for $200. That talk resulted in a project for the research center of which I was a part.

Lesson Learned:

Most people's judgment of the value of a product or service is based on the price they must pay to acquire it, however unrelated it may be to its value.

BELL: A BLACK AND WHITE CASE

The President of Bell of Pennsylvania – then a part of AT&T – asked the Busch (research) Center at Wharton to look at the following problem. Nearly 50% of the company's employees were black but less than 1% of its supervisory and management personnel were black. We were asked to determine what kind of training would equip black employees to move up the hierarchy and to provide it.

Since we were heavily involved in the development of a black neighborhood (Mantua) we welcomed the questions. After some preliminary thought, we met with Bell's Vice President of Personnel and a few of his staff. We explained what we wanted to do: to examine the educational records of 500 black women employed by Bell and compare them with the records of 500 white women *in the same positions*. We also wanted to do the same thing for 500 black and white male employees.

The Vice President told us that such a comparison was not necessary. He assured us that we could safely assume that male and female black employees were functionally illiterate and ignorant of even elementary arithmetic. We said we needed to determine if this was true and measure the gap between black and white employees by examining the personnel records of those in our sample. He told us these records were held in three different locations. We said this would not be an obstacle. He then said we could not be given access to these records. We explained that we could not conduct the study without such access. He continued to withhold it. The contract was aborted; we did not go ahead.

By chance I was in New York City shortly thereafter and ran into an AT&T executive whom I knew. He told me he had heard of our project at Bell of PA. Then I told him that the contract had been canceled and why. He was angry about this and told me to expect possible reactivation of the contract.

About a week later I was told the contract had been reactivated and we would be given access to the personnel records we wanted. We laboriously collected and analyzed those records. We found that black females had 1½ years more equivalent education than their white counterparts, and black males had about ¾ of a year more education than white males in the same positions.

From this we concluded that there *was* a need for remedial education but that it should be given to whites in supervisory and managerial positions. We argued that it was their attitudes towards blacks rather than any deficiencies in the blacks that held them back. This conclusion was rejected by the Vice President of Personnel and the contract was canceled again. This time it was not resuscitated.

About a year later black Bell employees took out a class action suit against Bell alleging racial prejudice in the workplace. The case went to court and the black employees won. They were given the largest cash settlement by the court that had been given to any minority group up to that time.

LESSON LEARNED:
It is easier to attribute one's deficiencies to others than to face them in oneself.

Mantua: Fish that got Tanked

One of the earliest requests for assistance we received from the Young Great Society in Mantua was bizarre. The elementary school had been given a very large fish tank. It planned to set it up in the entrance lobby of the school. It had been promised fish but needed 500 gallons of pond water to fill the tank. This is what we were asked to obtain.

I called the University's botanical gardens and asked if they could supply the water. They could. Now the problem was how to transport the water from the gardens to the school in Mantua: at least ten miles. I called someone I knew in the Gulf Refinery in Philadelphia and asked if the company had a tank truck that could be used for this purpose. Much to my surprise, it did.

Arrangements were made for pickup and delivery of the pond water. It was put in the tank and the fish added. But when the school's staff arrived the next morning they found water and dead fish all over the floor. The tank had broken during the night.

It was important for us to have shown a willingness to try to do whatever the neighborhood asked us to do. Fortunately we were not sent chasing pond water again but in this case, as in many others, we learned a great deal about our ability to do things for which we had no knowledge or expertise.

Lesson Learned:

Determination to respond to a request that initially requires knowledge one does not have is one of the best ways to expand one's knowledge.

MANTUA IN MONTE CARLO

Herman Wrice and I were invited to address an annual meeting of the Young Presidents' Organization (YPO) to be held in Monte Carlo. We accepted enthusiastically. Within a short time of arriving it became apparent that Herman, who was black, was an oddity in Monte Carlo because of his color. During the days that followed I was frequently asked who Herman was. I told them he was the chief of a Central African tribe. To make this more believable, Herman and I tried to find a dashiki that he could wear, but we had no such luck. He was treated as something special throughout the meetings.

One night Herman and I decided to visit the gambling casino to see what it was like. There was a checking facility in the entry lobby which we used for the things we were carrying. After about a half hour tour of the casino we returned to the checkout counter to retrieve our things before leaving. On the floor directly in front of the counter was a huge wad of American bills, the outside one being for $100. It was held together by a thick rubber band.

Herman picked it up and handed it to the girl behind the counter. She was amazed and asked Herman why he did not keep it for his own use. Herman said that the person who had dropped would probably return looking for it and he would undoubtedly need the money more than Herman did.

The convention closed with a banquet held in the casino's ballroom. There was a slightly raised platform at one end of the ballroom with one table on the side for speakers and another in the center for YPO executives and the Prince (Rainier) and Princess (Grace Kelly). The Prince and Princess sat at opposite ends of their table.

Herman and I were seated at the speaker's table. Sigmund Freud's nephew, Clement, a food critic for a British newspaper, sat directly across from Herman. He was clearly drunk. He began to address insulting racial remarks to Herman. I butted in and we were just getting a real brouhaha going when a voice at the entry to the ballroom boomed out, "Herman". It was Jack Kelly, Grace's brother, who was a councilman from Philadelphia and a friend of Herman's.

He came to the table and took Herman over to the center table and seated him next to Grace. He also took me over to the central table and sat me beside the Prince. We had a wonderful time and Mr. Freud was obviously greatly embarrassed. The next morning Herman received a lengthy apology from him.

LESSON LEARNED:
The need for a resource increases with the amount one has.

Mantua in Puerto Rico

With support from the Anheuser-Busch Companies we put
on a course for twenty-one gang leaders drawn from the black
community of Mantua. They were enticed to attend by paying
them a salary to do so and allowing them to set the agenda.
The class met in a room in the College of Engineering of the
University of Pennsylvania during the summer when the building
was sparsely used. Shortly after it began, I received a call in my
office in the middle of the day telling me there was a crisis in
the building in which the class was held. I was told to come
immediately. It was about three blocks across the campus. I ran all
the way.

One of the class members had to use the washroom and he did
not know where it was. He left the class and wandered down the
hall to the first occupied office he saw. It was occupied by a young
secretary. He went in to ask her where the washroom was. Because
he carried a pistol in his belt and was wearing no jacket he looked
menacing to her. She screamed and people came running from all
directions. The class was disrupted and spilled into the hall.

We got the fuss settled and the class then agreed not to carry guns
to school.

About the second week of the class a deputation came to see me
and asked if a course in rapid reading could be provided. This was
a euphemism because most of them were functionally illiterate.
We arranged a class in remedial reading (not so labeled) that was
held in their own time in the evenings. They took it very seriously.

A week or so later another deputation asked for a course in
"mathematics". We arranged for a course in elementary arithmetic,
also given in their own time. This too was well attended and
appreciated.

At the end of the class its members wanted a graduation ceremony with caps and gowns and certificates given out by the President of the University. All this was arranged and went off without any difficulty. The class also wanted a formal prom. This too was arranged. All the class members came in tuxedos with their girl friends dressed in evening gowns with corsages. Several parents served as chaperons. It was a wonderful evening.

However, problems arose in connection with the class trip that they wanted. Because none of them had ever left Philadelphia, let alone the country, they wanted to go outside the United States. I asked August Busch III, if he would let us use a corporate jet to go abroad. He said we could not use one to go abroad but he would supply one to take the class anywhere in the United States.

The class huddled over this problem and decided on Puerto Rico because it was "foreign". Accompanied by two chaperons they were flown to San Juan. The next day I received a call from one of the chaperons asking if the plane could return and take the class back to Philadelphia. I asked why. It turned out they had not been aware that the natives spoke a foreign language. They felt isolated and disoriented. I asked the chaperons to try to work out a different solution.

I received a call the next day saying that everything was fine. They would remain for the week planned. I asked what had been done. They had gone into the local prison to play basketball with the inmates and did this every day of their visit. Language was not a barrier to the fun of the play. In fact, it seemed to add to it.

Lesson Learned:
Play has a universally understood language of its own.

Boycott in Atlanta

August Busch III, then CEO of Anheuser-Busch Companies, called me one day to tell me there was a boycott against his company's products in a particular region of Atlanta, Georgia. He asked if I could help determine its cause. I said I would try.

I consulted with Herman Wrice, a community leader in a disadvantaged area of Philadelphia called Mantua. I had been working closely with Herman for several years on development projects in his neighborhood. We had become close friends. Our joint effort was financed by Anheuser-Busch. Herman suggested sending two members of his staff to Atlanta to take up residence there temporarily. The task he gave them to serve as a cover was to negotiate baseball games between young people in Atlanta and Philadelphia.

They spent their first nights in neighborhood bars trying to identify the adults who ran the baseball league for young people. They found out who they were fairly quickly. Then they started meeting with these organizers, also in neighborhood bars. One night they mentioned that they had noticed the boycott of Anheuser-Busch products and wondered why it had been initiated. One of the men with whom they were negotiating identified himself as the instigator.

When asked why he had initiated the boycott, he told them, "Because my brother, who is employed by Anheuser-Busch in its Newark brewery, had asked me to do so". The Mantuans then asked why his brother had made such a request. The initiator of the boycott explained that his brother had asked the Newark brewery manager for financial support with attending night school at Rutgers University in order to study accounting. He had been turned down. Because of this he had requested the boycott to "get even with the company".

That night this information was telephoned to me in Philadelphia. I called August Busch the next day and passed the information on to him. He asked if I had any suggestions as to how the situation could be handled. Fortunately, early that morning I had discussed this with those involved in Atlanta and Herman. As they had advised I suggested a full-time scholarship be given to the disgruntled employee to attend Rutger's Business School.

August saw to it that this was done very quickly. The boycott was terminated the same day. That disgruntled Newark employee eventually earned a degree from Rutgers and went to work in the accounting department of the Newark Brewery.

LESSON LEARNED:
A boycott can be caused by a boy caught.

Contact: Avoiding Suicide

Our research center at The Wharton School, the Busch Center, often took on *pro bono* projects for non-profit organizations. One of these organizations was called CONTACT and was located in Harrisburg, the state capital of Pennsylvania. CONTACT provided a 24-hour telephone counseling service every day of every week to those contemplating suicide. Trained volunteers would answer the calls and try to talk the callers out of their intention to do away with themselves. They also offered to obtain continuing professional help for those who would accept it.

The United Way supported this organization financially but the level of support had been gradually reduced. CONTACT could not operate if another reduction took place, and one was contemplated. They asked us for help.

They hoped we could help them find other sources of support. We suggested that it would be preferable to find a way to make them self supporting so they would not be dependent on the charity of others. They agreed but could not imagine how to do this. We could. We suggested that for a fee they offer a 24-hour telephone answering service for doctors, companies and anyone who needed such an answering service. We pointed out that they already had the phones and personnel to answer such calls. It was just a matter of expanding their services. They did so and survived.

Lesson Learned:

Every resource has more than one use; it may be necessary to employ more than one of these uses to preserve another of them.

Imperial Oil: Organizing a New Business

As a result of some research we were doing for Imperial Oil, the wholly owned Canadian subsidiary of Exxon, we suggested to Robert Peterson, its CEO, that he create a division to produce and market gas liquids, for example, propane and butane. He did so and appointed Bill McAdam, a young member of the corporate planning department, as head of that unit. He also appointed eight others as heads of functionally defined departments reporting directly to McAdam. They all were older than McAdam and with more experience of gas liquids than McAdam had. This was a recipe for disaster, and it came.

McAdam, who had worked with us before, immediately set up a board consisting of his eight direct reports. Several months later he phoned me to say the board was a disaster. Its members devoted their meetings to political infighting and would not stick with an issue so as to reach a conclusion.

The meetings did nothing but generate ill will among the members. None of the members liked the board and would just as soon have it discontinued. McAdam asked me what could be done.

I arranged a meeting with the eight subordinates without McAdam present. The task I gave them was to make suggestions to McAdam that would enable them to do their jobs better. They came up with more than forty suggestions and prioritized them. Then they assigned responsibility to each of the eight for presenting several of the suggestions to McAdam in a face-to-face meeting.

Later, the presentations were made in a small conference room. McAdam immediately agreed to implement each of the first three suggestions and said they were very good ideas. He wished he had thought of them. At this point the oldest member of the group broke in and addressed McAdam: "You may not be aware of the fact that I resented your appointment as head of this unit. I felt I should have been given the job because I have more relevant experience than you have had and I'm older than you. Therefore, I've been doing everything I could to make you look bad in the hope you would be replaced and I would get the job. Listening to you in this meeting I've come to realize that you are a reasonable person and that you have the welfare of this unit and all of us in this room at heart. I'm sorry I have been acting the way I have. I want you to know that from here on I will cooperate with you and be supportive of you."

Bill McAdam replied by saying how pleased he was with that statement. He went one to say he had been aware of the efforts referred to and that he had been trying to get that manager removed and replaced. He then said he would discontinue that effort. At that point a number of confessions of disruptive and uncooperative behavior followed and promises were made to discontinue these practices.

By the end of the session the group had become a team working together for the good of the division. The board began to do what it was supposed to do. Performance of the division began to improve significantly.

LESSON LEARNED:
Being born again is not only a religious experience.

ANHEUSER-BUSCH WENT HEAVY ON LIGHT

Early in the 1960s we (the Case Operations Research Group) carried out some market research for Anheuser-Busch. The objective was to determine whether advertising affected sales, and if so, how much. A detailed account of this work was subsequently published. Among other things, this research involved interviewing heavy, moderate, light and non beer drinkers. As an unintended by-product we found that there was a potential market for a low-calorie beer. I sent a memo to this effect to the elder Mr. Busch, then CEO. He sent my message to the brew master for reply. The reply said that most of the calories in beer were contained in its alcohol. Therefore, the only way to reduce the calories in beer was to lower its alcohol content. This, he wrote, had been tried in what was known as 3.2 percent beer. It had been a failure. He discarded my suggestion.

Two years later, in 1963, in another market study we found the same indication: that there was a large market for a low-calorie beer. Once again I sent a memo to this effect to Mr. Busch, and once again he forwarded it to the brew master. His reply contained the same information as his earlier response and he discarded the suggestion once again.

In the early 1970s, about ten years after my first memo had been written, Miller introduced "Lite" beer with lower calories than normal beer. It was an instant success. Anheuser-Busch was caught "with its pants down". Its brew master could not let this go unchallenged. In about six months Anheuser-Busch had developed "Bud Light". With a very costly but creative advertising campaign it eventually caught up with Miller and surpassed it. The delay had cost the company dearly.

LESSON LEARNED:

Although it is better to be late than never, it is better to be too early than too late.

From Case to Penn

In August 1964 all but one member of the Operations Research faculty of Case Institute of Technology in Cleveland, together with a large part of their students, moved to The Wharton School of the University of Pennsylvania. All the sponsors of their research projects decided to move with them.

The selection of The Wharton School as their new home was the result of a process begun in February of that year. The new President Elect of Case had instituted policies that I found incompatible with my educational and research objectives. Therefore, I submitted my resignation. The next day all but one of the members of the OR faculty submitted their resignations. On learning about this impending collective departure, representatives of the student body asked that they be considered as part of a possible collective move to another institution of higher learning. We agreed to start a search for a new home, but if we could not find one by May, we would go our separate ways.

The search began by sending letters to people we knew in 18 different universities announcing our departure from Case and asking if their institution had any interest in our joining it. We received positive responses from three University business schools: The University of California at Berkeley, Washington University in St. Louis and The University of Pennsylvania (Penn). I was the only member of the faculty who was an alumnus of any of these institutions (Penn). As a result, I disqualified myself from the selection process that was developed. A group of the faculty members arranged a visit to each of the three institutions. Then they produced a recommendation for a new home: The Wharton School of The University of Pennsylvania. I then had responsibility for the final negotiation of the move. It went easily because of the cooperation of Keith Glennan, the departing president of Case, and Gaylord Harnwell, the President of Penn. The move took place on the Friday before Labor Day. On the Tuesday after Labor Day we were operating out of Penn.

When leaving Case we could not legally solicit a corresponding move by our research sponsors. However, we could notify them of our impending move and we did. All but one of them (whose project was almost complete) expressed the desire to move with us. Our projects and faculty became part of the Management Science Center at Penn. Academically we joined the Department of Statistics in The Wharton School which was renamed the Department of Statistics and Operations Research when we became a part of it.

In the late 1960s I became aware of the growing importance of systems thinking. I, therefore, proposed an option within the OR program of a systems major. It was rejected by the relevant faculty committee. I resubmitted in each of the next two years and I was joined by four other members of the OR faculty. We submitted a proposal for an experimental graduate program in the Systems Sciences. The experimental department and its academic program were approved but not the name that we had proposed. There was a Systems Engineering program in the Engineering College which argued that Systems Sciences would cause confusion. We then settled for Social Systems Sciences which came to be known as "S Cubed (S3)". Six years later the department was changed from its experimental status to a regular department in The Wharton School.

The new department created an academic program that did not have most of the characteristics expected of it. It had no entrance, only exit, requirements. Applicants were evaluated by a student committee. There were no required courses. Students designed their own graduate program and presented it to a faculty committee for approval. Students were able to select any courses given in the University, any learning and research cells they wanted, and independent study. It was easy for them to change their programs subsequently by reappearing before the faculty committee with their proposals.

The principal pedagogical instruments were learning cells and research cells. Learning cells consisted of a group of students with one or more faculty member(s) who wanted to learn and explore a specified subject. Each cell organized its own learning process. In addition, students were required to work on projects in what came to be called The Busch Center. These consisted of real problems confronting sponsoring and paying organizations. Small groups of students could form research cells in which, together with faculty member(s), they tried to consolidate what they were learning in the research projects.

A large number of students were employed by the Busch Center. They received a relatively handsome stipend in addition to coverage of their tuition fees. But they had to work hard. Since most of their projects were for corporations and government agencies, a great deal of travel and away-from-home time was involved. It was a wonderful experience, providing unique learning opportunities for the students, who were essentially in an apprentice relationship with one or more faculty member(s). Others in The Wharton School resented the size of the stipend we gave to our students. My good friend, William Gomberg (now deceased), professor of labor-management relations, organized a faculty committee to take up the issue of student compensation.

Immediately after the committee was formed I was asked to appear before it. When I appeared, the committee was draped around a conference table with Gomberg at the far end and my seat at the near end. Gomberg opened the session by asking me if I knew what the mission of the committee was. I said that I did. He then asked what I thought of its desire to equalize student compensation across departments and schools. I said I agreed with it. Gomberg said I must have a misunderstanding of its objective. (He knew I was at odds with his opinion on the issue.) I said he was the one who misunderstood. I agreed to equalization of student compensation at the level at which we compensated our students.

He said this was not feasible because much of the University's research was sponsored by the National Science Foundation. And, he added, the Foundation placed an upper limit on the compensation of students involved in their projects – a limit that was below what we were paying. I told him he should notify the Foundation of this fact because it was obviously unaware of such a limit. We had two contracts with the Foundation at the time, and the Foundation knew exactly what we were paying our students. The committee's collective face turned red. I was dismissed shortly afterwards and I never heard anything further about it.

Our department was governed by a Committee of the Whole on which every student, faculty and staff member had an equal vote. The committee's responsibility covered selection of new faculty and staff members, separation of existing faculty or staff members, scheduling and offerings of courses and cells.

I personally only ever had one serious disagreement with this Committee of the Whole. Our program led to a PhD degree. We had no Master's program. However, we did offer a Master's degree to those students who were not considered good enough for the PhD, but good enough for a lesser degree. It was a sort of consolation prize. But the Master's degree required a thesis, just as the PhD did. Three students wanted to remove that requirement. Every time they brought it up before the governing body I argued against it and succeeded in preventing its passage.

Once, when I was on a relatively extended trip for a project, the students called a meeting of the Committee of the Whole and passed the motion to eliminate the required Master's thesis. When I returned, a committee of three very self-satisfied students came into my office and told me what they had done. I said nothing but while they stood there I wrote out my resignation from the department and gave it to them. They objected saying I was not abiding by democratic rule. I said I reserved the ultimate human right, the right to emigrate when the conditions of staying were intolerable. I could not rescind their decision but I did not have to accept it.

They asked me to withhold my resignation until they called a follow-up meeting of the Committee of the Whole. In that meeting we discussed the reasons the students wanted to eliminate the thesis requirement. Through discussion we found a way to allay their concerns while keeping the requirement. I withdrew my resignation. This was the only time the students tried political maneuvering to get approval for something they wanted.

Of our many departures from common practices there was one that the university not only approved of, but took credit for. This was the relationship we developed with the nearby black neighborhood of Mantua. This relationship was devoted to developing the neighborhood's ability to satisfy its needs and desires. The effort – led by the neighborhood's leader, Herman Wrice – attracted a great deal of attention because of its accomplishments. His anti-drug program was so successful that it was adopted by 62 other cities in the United States.

Our relationship with Mantua was exploited when the community initiated a vigorous demonstration against the university's policy of taking over land in its domain. We were asked by the university to negotiate a settlement. We negotiated with Herman Wrice and not surprisingly reached agreement quickly. The community got what it wanted and the university incurred no great loss. But it received a great deal of favorable publicity in return.

In many respects, the S3 Department was treated as the black sheep in the Wharton family; this despite the fact that our graduates had more job offers and a higher starting salary than any other graduates of Wharton. This led to a critical problem with a newly appointed Dean of the Wharton School, Russell Palmer. He was the first non academic appointed to that post. He came from an accounting firm which he had headed. He could not tolerate a variety greater than one. He made a number of efforts to make us conform to school standards and practices which, fortunately, we successfully rejected. He then decided to attack us in a different way.

At a national meeting of Business School Deans and CEOs of prominent corporations, Palmer sat next to Jim Rinehart, CEO of Clark Equipment Corporation. Palmer was not aware of my relationship with Jim, which went far beyond that of provider and client. We were close friends. Palmer asked Jim if he was familiar with Wharton. Jim said he was, primarily through his work with me. Palmer then revealed that I was one his main problems. He said there was no one capable of succeeding me and therefore he would have to eliminate the department when I retired. My (then compulsory) retirement was two years off. Jim let me know about this conversation the next day. It was no surprise, so I decided to let it ride.

A short while later the Dean of the Business School at Erasmus University in Holland, Jacob de Smit, was invited to a meeting of Business School Deans. Palmer sat next to him. Palmer did not know he had been a student of mine a number of years earlier. Then Palmer repeated his intention to disband the department on my retirement. Jacob related this to me a day or so later.

I thought that perhaps I should take some action. I consulted with the Vice Provost, Richard Clelland, who was an old friend and my successor as chairman of the Statistics and OR Department. I relayed information to him about Palmer's two conversations and asked for advice on how to handle it. With the best of intentions Dick spoke to Palmer about this. Palmer called me into his office and told me that he knew of my report on the two conversations. He denied that they had taken place. I responded by saying that obviously either he or my two friends were lying. Since I had known them for many years and they had no reason to lie to me, but he did, I took their word to be true.

I decided that I could not work under his direction. So I resigned from Wharton two years before I had to. I did so unilaterally. But the day after I announced this, a number of faculty members and students spoke to me about trying another collective move. We decided to create a corporation that would provide education and research assistance to organizations. One of the students suggested a name for it: INTERACT.

Palmer warned me about soliciting our clients to move. I told him I was aware of the legal requirements. However, I could and did prepare an announcement of our conversion into INTERACT. I sent a copy to Palmer and one to each of our sponsors. All our clients except one immediately contacted us and said they wanted to move with us. They did. The corporation was created and flourished for a number of years.

Lesson Learned:

In a bureaucracy the only thing harder than starting something new is stopping something old.

Iran: Cigarette Smoke Gets in their Eyes

I was sent to Iran by the United Nations to assist the Minister of Consumer Affairs. The problem on which he wanted assistance had to do with the sale of American Cigarettes. The sale of cigarettes was one of the largest sources of income to the government. Although the government produced a number of different brands of cigarettes, American Cigarettes enjoyed a large share of the market. They were sold through tobacco shops that the government had licensed.

Smuggled American cigarettes were being sold illegally on the street by unlicensed vendors who offered them at a lower price than that offered by the licensed stores. As a result the government's income from cigarette sales was decreasing significantly.

The government had offered a reward for information leading to the arrest and conviction of the smugglers. But it had turned up very few of them. The minister asked me what size reward should the government offer in order to get a large number of them identified.

Before turning to his question we investigated the costs associated with the sale of both the smuggled and legitimately sold cigarettes. We found that the smuggled cigarettes cost less to bring to the consumer than the legitimate ones and the profit realized by the smugglers and their salesmen was greater then that obtained by the government and its distributors. The smugglers were able to buy the cigarettes in Kuwait tax free and, therefore, at a lower price than the government could get them for directly from the United States. So we suggested that the government handle the cigarette business exactly as the smugglers did and buy their cigarette supplies in Kuwait. If they did they would have even lower costs than the smugglers and, as a result, even larger profits.

The government did so and realized increased profit.

LESSON LEARNED:

Virtuous does not mean smart and evil does not mean dumb.

US Brewers Association and Solid Waste

We had convinced the US Brewers Association to initiate an anti-litter campaign. We suggested "Unlitter a litter bit today" as the slogan. The association consulted its advertising agency which changed the slogan to "Pitch in". They planned an advertising campaign and decided to place litter receptacles around the center of a few selected cities. The question of assessing their efficacy came to us. We decided to run an experiment in Philadelphia.

We selected two stretches on Chestnut Street in the main shopping area in the city center. We counted the amount of litter before doing anything to the blocks to be used. Then we installed litter bins in one of the stretches, three per block, so that one could be seen from any position in the block.

We then counted the amount of litter at the end of each of several days. The amount of litter added each day was proportional to the amount that was there at the beginning of the day. There was virtually no littering where the sidewalks were completely devoid of it. The more litter there was at the beginning of the day, the more would be added during that day. This was not a surprising result but it did make it possible to locate the right number of receptacles so as to virtually eliminate litter in otherwise heavily littered areas.

Lesson Learned:
Waste baskets distributed around can reduce litter but not eliminate it; only public morality can do this, as in Holland.

IBM: Office Arrangement

Shortly after IBM had moved its headquarters to Armonk, New York, I visited it in connection with some research we were doing for the company. Whilst walking down a hall I came across an old friend who worked for IBM. He asked if this was the first time I had been in the building. I told him it was. He invited me to see his office.

His office was elegantly furnished with expensive modern furniture. The desk faced away from an outside wall that was made entirely of glass. His visitor's chair was on the other side of his desk facing the glass wall. The sun was shining through that wall and blinded me. I could not see my friend because of the glare.

I remarked about this and said it could easily be corrected by repositioning the desk, its chair, and the visitor's chair. My friend said, "Let's do it". We did.

The next day when I was back in my office I received a phone call from my friend at IBM. He told me that when he had come to his office that morning the furniture was back in its original position and there was a warning on his desk. It said that his prerogatives did not include changing the arrangement of the furniture in his office.

Lesson Learned:

Sometimes it is better to do the wrong thing right than to do the right thing.

Anheuser-Busch's Gardens

When Anheuser-Busch (A-B) built its Tampa brewery, the elder Mr. Augustus Busch, then CEO, had moved his collection of exotic birds to the grounds surrounding the brewery. They were set up in a small but beautifully arranged garden. It was open to the public at no cost. A tour of the brewery was offered to those visitors who wanted it. There was also a Hospitality House where visitors could relax, sample the company's beers, and learn something about the brewing process. The number of visitors grew rapidly. It became the principal tourist attraction in the Tampa-St. Petersburg area.

Later, when the Los Angeles brewery was built, Mr. Busch wanted to have a similar attraction built there. The company's board turned it down because, it said, the cost of maintaining the Tampa attraction was very high.

Mr. Busch asked me to find out how much the garden was worth to the company and, if possible, to find out how to generate income to cover its cost.

The most obvious possibility that occurred to us was to charge for parking. Anheuser-Busch's management feared that this would significantly reduce attendance. We were asked to find out if this was so. We identified a number of urban attractions around the United States where a charge for parking had been introduced after a period in which it had been provided at no cost. These included zoos, museums and botanical gardens. We found that without exception attendance had increased after a charge for parking was introduced. This convinced Anheuser-Busch's management. A charge for parking was introduced at the Tampa Gardens and attendance continued to increase at more than its previous rate. It appeared that the value placed on a visit to an attraction was proportional to the cost associated with it.

We conducted a study of how the visitors' time was spent at the various parts of the gardens. We found that, on the average, visitors were exposed to 11 minutes of company advertising of a very high quality. Then, using the number and type of visitors, we determined the cost per minute of this exposure. It turned out to be considerably less than it cost to obtain the same exposure through television. Furthermore, it was much more effective advertising.

Mr. Busch was delighted with this finding. He used it to get approval of his plan for Los Angeles. It was not successful. Fortunately for us, we were not involved with it in any way.

Our study of how visitors spent their time at the Gardens showed a considerable drop in attendance between 11.00am and 1.00pm, when visitors left for lunch. Therefore, we suggested that a restaurant be added – one that would be accessible from the Gardens. At that time Mr. Busch had just married a Swiss woman whose family had operated a famous restaurant in Switzerland. Mr. Busch reproduced that restaurant in the Brewery grounds. It did not attract a large number of visitors. We were asked to find out why. The answer was easy to find. The restaurant was too luxurious, too costly and too time consuming for lunch, especially with a number of children in tow. A large percentage of visitors had children with them.

Using these results Mr. Busch then had a German beer garden built inside the Gardens. This "Festhaus" served German food and beer in big mugs at long community tables. It featured a German "oompah" band and German folk dancers. Food was provided in a cafeteria style and inexpensively. The "Festhaus" was a huge success and it succeeded in adding to attendance at around midday.

Eventually an admission charge was introduced and gift shops were spread around the Gardens along with a number of other attractions such as thrill rides and craft shops. Attendance continued to grow through all of this.

Later, Anheuser-Busch acquired land outside of Williamsburg on which to build a brewery. The company also decided to build a major family attraction there. At that time, I had just returned from Holland where I had been on vacation with my wife and three small children. They had fallen in love with Maduradam in The Hague. This attraction consisted of miniaturized versions of the major features one could see around Holland. It included houses, churches, an airport, a sea port, canals and so on. Everything was in the open. Traffic moved through the port, planes taxied on a runway, ships moved in the waterway, singing came from the church, and so on.

I suggested to Mr. Busch that he visit Maduradam. He did and came away from it with a decision about what to do with the Williamsburg Gardens. He would build small villages with full-size attractions from around the world – French, German, English, Italian, etc. This was done and the Gardens were a huge success.

Under the leadership of Mr. Busch's son (August Busch III) the company expanded its entertainment business through a number of acquisitions. It already owned the St. Louis Cardinals, a major league baseball team. It acquired Sea World, Cypress Gardens, Boardwalk and Baseball, and Adventure Island, a water based attraction. It also built Sesame Place in the Philadelphia area. It later sold some of these attractions but nevertheless became the third largest family entertainment provider in the country. Disney was first and United Artists was second.

Lesson Learned:
It is easier, but costlier, to follow than to lead.

Anheuser-Busch and Brooks Brothers

I was meeting with August Busch III and Ed Vogel, Vice President of Marketing, in New York City at the Hotel Pierre in their usual suite. We had started early in the morning, had lunch in the room and continued well into the afternoon. About mid afternoon August and Ed wanted to go out and walk a bit "to get rid of the cobwebs".

I joined them in a walk down Fifth Avenue. We came to a Brooks Brothers store. They decided they would like to stop in while they were there. We entered the store and took an elevator up to the top floor, which consisted of a luxurious lounge. The salesmen there greeted them by name and obviously knew them well. They were shown bolts of material that could be used to make suits. They each ordered several suits. Their measurements were clearly on file, so they could leave after arranging to have the suits sent to them once they were made. There was no exchange of money but the salesman did say what the price per suit would be.

August suggested I buy a suit while we were there. I pointed out that he had just spent more than I made in a month. He did not press me to make a purchase. It was a long time before I earned enough to buy a suit at Brooks Brothers and then it was ready-made, not tailored as theirs were.

Lesson Learned:

What suits one may not suit another.

C&O: Ideas Locked Out

Occasionally I would meet with the Board of Directors at Chesapeake and Ohio Railroad (C&O) to report on the work my colleagues at Case and I were doing. On one occasion we had been asked if we could help with scheduling a classification yard. I said I thought we could. Then I was invited to discuss the way we intended to go about it with the Corporation's board.

The meeting was in the boardroom. I spoke from the head of the table. Seated immediately to my left was the 85- year-old treasurer of the company. Shortly after I had completed my presentation and the discussion of it had begun, he asked me if I had ever worked on a railroad. I said not. He then asked if my father had ever worked on a railroad. Again I said not. He asked if anyone in my family had ever worked on a railroad. Once again I said not. He then asked why, with no relevant experience, I thought I could recognize good or bad railroad practices. I answered by telling a story.

The Guggenheim Museum in New York City had been designed by Frank Lloyd Wright. After it was completed, Louis Mumford, then the best-known architectural critic in the United States, blasted the building in print. This started a bitter exchange between Wright and Mumford. The New York Academy of Science decided to exploit the situation by asking the two of them to engage in a public debate. They accepted.

At the appropriate time and place they both appeared, seated on stage with the Chairman of the session sitting between them. The Chairman opened the meeting. After a few initial remarks, he said that, in deference to age, he would ask Wright to make the opening statement. Wright arose and walked to the front of the stage, turned and addressed Mumford. He asked, "Have you ever designed a building?" Mumford indicated by shaking his head that he hadn't. Wright then asked, "Then why do you think you are qualified to criticize the design of another?" Mumford arose and said: "Mr. Wright, I never laid an egg but I can tell the difference between a good one and a bad one."

The old man to my left then said that a story about eggs had nothing to do with the operation of a railroad. Fortunately, the other managers present did not agree with him and we got a contract to do the study. But I learned then how ineffective argument by analogy could be.

LESSON LEARNED:
Some minds cannot be penetrated even by an idea.

C&O: From Russ to Professor

Whenever I met with the board of the Chesapeake and Ohio Railroad C&O board I dressed in what I thought was an appropriate way, with a jacket and tie. These meetings occurred with sufficient frequency so that I was usually addressed informally by my first or last name. One day when I was working in my office at Case, John Kusick, the Vice President of Finance, called me and said I was wanted at a board meeting going on at that moment. Case was about a 15-minute drive from C&O headquarters.

I was in a sweat suit and I told him I would have to go home to change my clothes. He replied there was no time for that. "Come immediately," he said.

I did and, on arrival, I entered the room occupied by the well-dressed members of C&O's board. Throughout that meeting, for the first time, they all called me "Professor".

LESSON LEARNED:
As Mark Twain observes, "Clothes make the man". However, they also affect the whole way he is perceived by the world.

Mantua: Honky in Chicago

Forrest Adams, one of the activists in Mantua, invited me to go along with him to a meeting in Chicago. It was a meeting called by the nationally known black leader Floyd McKissick. The meeting was held in a former motion picture theater on the south side of the city. When we entered the theater I looked around and saw only one other Caucasian. So I asked Forrest if we could sit on the back row so as to be as inconspicuous as possible. We found seats in the middle of that row.

The light flickered and McKissick came out on the stage and stood at the podium. Using a microphone he called the meeting to order. As he began his opening statement he noticed me and stopped. Then, pointing, he asked, "Who let that honky in here?"

Forrest stood up and all the eyes in the auditorium focused on him and me. He slowly surveyed the theater from left to right and then called out, "Floyd, I don't see no honky". That was the end of it. The meeting proceeded as planned.

LESSON LEARNED:
Color is in the eye of the beholder not in the skin of the beheld.

Mars and Mexican Dog Food

The CEO of Mars asked the Busch Center at Wharton to look at a factory his corporation had in Southern California. It was not performing as well as he thought it should. Several of my colleagues and I went out for an initial meeting with the plant's management. The managers told us their major problem was the work force. It was made up exclusively of Mexican immigrants who could not speak or read English. Since the managers could not speak Spanish there was a wide gap between management and the work force. There was no effective communication between them.

The managers said they felt the workforce was hostile to them. They had tried several times to show the workforce that they cared about them. They cited as an example a cafeteria they had built within the plant for the workforce. Before it was built most of the workers either brought their lunch or bought food from a small car-pulled trailer that parked outside the plant and from which Mexican food was sold. After the cafeteria was opened the workers continued to bring their own food or buy from the trailer. The cafeteria was virtually deserted every day. We asked the managers if they had involved the workforce in the design of the cafeteria and the decision as to what kind of foods it would serve. They said they hadn't. We then said it was this fact that kept the cafeteria from being used. It was not perceived by the workers as their cafeteria but as management's.

We suggested that they arrange for a meeting between us and the leaders of the workforce. They said they would do so but we should be aware of the fact that the workers only spoke Spanish which none of us understood. We told them we would take care of this deficiency. We then arranged to meet the group of workers at a specified time in a small conference room at the plant site.

Unbeknown to them we brought with us Elsa Vergara, a young Mexican graduate student in our program, who also spoke very good English. All the workers were deliberately gathered in the meeting room before we arrived. When we did, Elsa went in first. She immediately began to thank them for coming in Spanish. They all rose and gathered around her and began to talk in Spanish. We learned later that they were comparing familiarity with different communities in Mexico and that they had even found some Mexicans they knew in common.

The chatter went on for some time while we English-speakers sat quietly. After a while they broke up and seated themselves with us around the table. Then the one who was apparently the leader asked me in good but broken English what this meeting was about. I remarked on his English and the fact that management had told us none of them could communicate in that language. They laughed and then in English made us promise we would not let management know they could communicate in our language. We made the promise but asked for an explanation.

They told us that the managers knew nothing about running a plant such as theirs. Therefore, if they allowed management to manage it the plant would eventually fold. They kept it going by pretending not to understand management.

After that meeting we kept our word and did not let the managers know what we had learned. We suggested that they ask the workforce to put on a course in Spanish that they would attend in the evenings. We also set about studying the way management had been trying to run the plant. We concluded that the workers were right: the managers would destroy it with their efforts to control it. We reported these results back to corporate headquarters.

Unfortunately we had no further communication with either corporate headquarters or the plant's management. We did learn that the plant continued to operate even after the company had built a new one in the East. We also learned indirectly that some of the managers had been replaced.

LESSON LEARNED:

Ignorance is sometimes the best defense against know-it-alls.

ALCOA: Labor Versus Management and Vice Versa

ALCOA Tennessee (AT) was ALCOA's largest operation in the 1970s. It was established in 1906 and consisted of three very large factories, each separately located for safety's sake in case of bombing. There were also a number of smaller supporting facilities and parts of the hydroelectric system in the Tennessee Valley. There were about 6,000 employees with several thousand hourly paid workers who were members of the United Steel Workers Union, Local 309, the union's largest ocal. It was the largest employer of unionized labor in the state.

There had been labor-management disputes from the beginning, including a number of wildcat strikes. In 1978 there was a particularly bad one in which part of a factory was blown up and several workers were hurt. As a result, in early 1979, ALCOA's executives (headquartered in Pittsburgh) decided to close the operation by December 31, 1984.

A new director, Dick Ray, was appointed; his task was to close the place with minimal disruption. I had met Dick, an American, in Australia on one of my visits there. I was also working with the CEO and President of ALCOA on an unrelated project at the time. Dick came to see me at Wharton. He said that his task was to officiate at a wake. This was of little interest to him. He would like to change the executives' decision and keep AT open. He asked me to help. What a challenge! He assigned Frank Cormia, his chief industrial engineer, to work with my colleague, Bill Deane, and me.

In early meetings with the senior management of AT I expressed the need to meet with the union and involve it in discussions about the problem. I was repeatedly told, "No", because it would be a waste of time. The way the union was described made its leaders sound like communist ogres. My colleague and I persisted. After several months of focusing exclusively on what management could do on its own – which clearly would never be enough – we were permitted to meet with the union's leadership.

Some meeting! It took place at the Local's headquarters with about 15 union officials present. We opened by saying we were there in the hope of setting up a dialogue between them and management about the closing of the AT operation. They responded by heaping invective on AT's management. In their eyes management consisted of a bunch of fascists. With this one exception they talked about management exactly like management talked about them. They told me that ALCOA's executives had threatened to close the operation in the past but had never followed through. I told them that I was working in Pittsburgh and could assure them they intended to do so this time. Nevertheless, they asked why they should believe me, especially since I was being paid by management. I told them it was a lot less risky for them to do so than not. If they assumed the operation would not be closed and it was, the cost to the union would be much greater than if they assumed the operation would be closed and it wasn't. I told them they could ask several other unions with which we had worked. We told them not to trust us, but test us continuously. This surprised them, and they responded to it positively. Eventually they agreed to meeting with AT's management if the Local's executives could set the conditions.

They agreed to a three-day meeting to be held at the hotel of their choice in Nashville, Tennessee. There would be nine union executives present and an equal number of AT managers. The two of us from Wharton were also to be present. The dates were specified. I called Dick Ray from the meeting room and obtained his agreement to the conditions. We all shook hands and left. After a brief meeting with AT's management, we returned to our offices at the University in Philadelphia. We left both parties very skeptical about the meeting's success. The next morning there was a call waiting for me from the president of the Local. He told me the meeting was off. Naturally, I asked why. He said that management had changed the hotel from the one that the union had designated and had done so without consulting them. I asked him to hold the line while I called Dick Ray for an explanation. He agreed. When I got Dick Ray on the phone and told him what was happening he professed no knowledge of the change. He told me he had assigned responsibility for making the arrangements to his Human Resources manager. I asked him to call that manager into his office and find out what had happened. I kept the line with the union president open. The HR manager entered Dick Ray's office. I could hear the conversation that followed. The hotel the Local had specified was completely full on the designated dates, so he had made arrangements with another hotel. I asked why he had not consulted the Local in making this decision. He said that he didn't think it was necessary. I pointed out that it was precisely that kind of thinking that was at the root of AT's problem. I offered to make the arrangements if the Local would agree. The Local's president (Tim), who had been told the reason for the infraction of the agreement, agreed. The meeting was back on.

No further problems. Early on the morning of the meeting Bill Deane and I went to the meeting room before any arrivals. There was a long table with nine seats on each side and a chair at each end. We made signs with names of all the attendants and then arranged them with each labor representative sitting next to a manager, alternating around the two sides on the table. Bill and I were to sit at the two ends of the table.

There was a sideboard with breakfast foods on it. We stood by this sideboard waiting for the first arrivals. They were two union executives. While one remained chatting with us the other rearranged the seating with all union people on one side of the table and all managers on the other. He then joined us. Without saying anything I went back to the table and restored the original arrangement.

The union executive who had changed the seating assured me my arrangement would not work. I said we would try it and see. Next several managers entered the room. One of them went to the table and rearranged the seating as the union executive had. Once again I changed it back.

When everyone had arrived they took their seats with obvious discomfort. Nevertheless, we started the meeting. For the first few hours each side unloaded its grievances with the other. Stories of management "atrocities" told by union executives went back to an episode involving one of their fathers in 1906. We let the resentment and mud slinging continue unabated until shortly before lunch.

I then read a passage from the operation's newspaper that criticized the Local and heaped invective on its leadership. I asked managers present if it believed all the things that were written about the Local. With embarrassment Dick Ray said, "No". He said it was part of the "game". The Local members basked while I chastised the managers for thinking their conflict between with the union was a game. I then turned the tables and read a corresponding passage from the Local's newspaper. The Local's executives confessed that it was an exaggeration of their views. While I chastised them the managers gloated.

Then I asked if the group wanted to continue playing that "game", which would guarantee the closing of the operation, or wanted to try something that might keep it open. They agreed to the latter.

After lunch we went to work. Over the next two and a half days the two sides reached agreement to start using management boards at the bottom and top of the organization's hierarchy. At the bottom, each foreman was to create a board consisting of his subordinates that chose to be on that board. Their functions were planning for the unit from which they came, policy making for that unit, coordination of plans and policies of these lowest level units, and integrating them with higher level plans and policies, making quality of working life decisions that affected members of the boards, and advising the manager whose board it was on what he could do to improve their work and working life.

At the top, Dick Ray would create a board consisting of nine managers plus nine Local representatives chosen by the Local's board. They would have the same tasks as the boards at the "bottom". A joint statement then went out to all unionized employees of AT asking them to volunteer for their foreman's board. About 6% responded. The foremen were not given the option of saying they would not participate. As the "good" done by these boards became obvious to those employees who had not agreed to serve on their foreman's board, more and more of them came onto the boards. Over 90% of them eventually participated.

For the first six months after the boards were formed almost all the decisions were directed at improving the workers' quality of working life. Then they began to focus on productivity issues.

Here are two examples of their initial decisions. Each of the three large plants was surrounded by a grass lawn about 15 yards wide. There were picnic tables in these areas where the men could eat their lunches. Since TO had no food dispensing facilities, the workers either brought their own lunches or their wives brought their lunches to them. This was not difficult for the wives because most of the workers lived within walking distance of the plants in which they were employed. However, the wives were not allowed through the gates so the workers had to go out to get the lunches that had been brought to them, and then re-enter the grounds of the plants, leaving their wives outside. The first change the low level boards made was to allow their wives to enter the grounds with them and have lunch with them.

The second change was to have a family day on which the workers could bring their children to show them where their fathers worked and what they did. Management picked up on this and made a real festival of it. Lunch was served, games were provided for the kids, and souvenirs distributed. It was a huge success.

In the top board the union members asked for details on the operation's performance each month. Management began to provide detailed reports which contained financial statements that the union representatives could not understand. They asked for a course on corporate finance that would enable them to understand the reports being given to them. We put on such a course and the Local representatives became "finance literate". As a result, the discussions at these board meetings became more and more interesting and management began to appreciate the questions and inputs from union members. The implementation of short- and long-run plans was visibly improved as a result.

In the 18 months following installation of the boards, productivity increased dramatically. Pittsburgh headquarters became curious about what was going on "down there". The CEO and some of the vice presidents reporting to him decided to go down and find out for themselves. They notified AT of their impending visit.

AT's management went into a fluster over preparation for the visit. We suggested that they let the Local do it. It took a good deal of persuasion but TO's management finally agreed. The Local put on an amazing show that praised management for all it had done to improve relations. The union representatives took the ALCOA executives on a guided tour through the plants showing the improvements that had been made. The executives from Pittsburgh were amazed.

Shortly thereafter ALCOA's top executives reversed the decision to close AT and said they would invest heavily in modernizing the plant. All the boards had an input into the planning that followed. In the next year the Corporation put $250,000 into the plant and converted it into the most productive sheet aluminum producer in the world.

At the formal opening of the remodeled plants there was an impressive ceremony involving the Governor of Tennessee and all of ALCOA's senior management. The ceremony was planned and executed by the Local. In the ceremony the Union cited the meeting in Nashville as the turning point in plant performance and labor-management relations.

The quality movement in the United States did not deliver the improvements expected of it. To a large extent this was due to its focus on the wrong quality, the quality of products or services an enterprise provided. It should focus on the quality of working life. Where the quality of working life is good, productivity and quality of output will take care of themselves. Where it is not good, no artifacts (like chats or slogans) can make it work.

Lesson Learned:

A high quality of working life assures a high quality of everything else.

ALCOA: Diversification

Charles Parry, CEO of ALCOA, told me one day that he was interested in diversifying the corporation. When I asked him what kind of acquisitions he was interested in, he said he did not know. So he suggested that we, at Wharton, see what we could come up with. He assured me he would know what he did *not* want when he saw it. However, after some additional conversation it became clear he was interested in high technology companies. Therefore, we restricted our inquiries to enterprises of this type. Fortunately, we found two small companies on the West coast that had return rates considerably higher than ALCOA's. Parry was interested; ALCOA acquired them.

About a year later he wondered why the returns these companies yielded were considerably lower than they had been when the companies were acquired. We were asked to look into it. We found no reduction in expected income but we did find a significant increase in their costs: the overhead charge imposed by corporate headquarters. It was clear that these companies were better off out of ALCOA than in it. They received nothing of value to them from ALCOA. A while later ALCOA divested itself of these two companies.

Lesson Learned:
A successful acquisition is one that focuses on adding value to the acquired company rather than the acquiring company.

Mexican Time

I spent the 1975-76 academic year in Mexico at the National Autonomous University (UNAM). While there I worked on a number of projects for the government and a few for businesses. While working on these projects in and out of the University, I learned a great deal about the Mexican concept of time. It is valued much less than it is in the United States. Furthermore, it is used as an instrument to reflect seniority as perceived by the person waited for: the greater the difference in status, the greater the waiting time.

I was engaged on a project in the ministry responsible for public housing. The project was managed by a third level official, a Director General. He was a young man who had recently joined the government from McKinsey and Co. He was tremendously impressed by his importance and displayed it in many ways. The way that affected me most was the time he kept me waiting each time I had an appointment to see him. Thirty to forty-five minutes was the standard.

After being kept waiting several times when I could see that the only person in his office was his secretary, I complained to him. I explained that I had limited time in Mexico and was working on a number of different projects in addition to teaching. I could not afford to spend any of my time waiting. He apologized and assured me it would not be necessary in the future. I told him that in the future if I was kept waiting more than ten minutes I would leave.

Shortly thereafter I had an appointment with him. I was seated in his waiting room at the time of the appointment. His deputy came out of his office and came over to chat with me. It was a transparent effort to make me unaware of waiting. I told the deputy that despite his presence I would leave after ten minutes. When the ten minutes were up I rose and walked to the elevator. The deputy walked with me and asked me to be patient and wait. I ignored his request. Just as I reached the elevator the Director General came running down the hall towards me asking me to wait; he would see me now. I told him that he had exceeded my limit. If he wanted to meet with me he should call my secretary at the university and arrange an appointment there. He was furious, but I left when the elevator arrived. Later that day I received a call at the university saying that our contract for work with that agency had been terminated. I expected it but was not concerned. There was more than enough other work to keep me busy.

The next day I received a phone call from the Deputy Minister to whom the Director General reported. He asked if I could work on a project for him. I said I could but told him of my collision with one of his Director Generals. He said he was aware of it and sympathized with me. He disliked the Director's arrogance as much as I did.

Lesson Learned:
The time one is kept waiting in Mexico is proportional to the gap in status between the one waiting and the one waited for, as perceived by the one waited for.

MEXICO: CLASS SCHEDULES, FACT OR FICTION

At the scheduled time, I went to my first class at the National Autonomous University of Mexico, where I was to spend my sabbatical year (1975-76). When I arrived the classroom was empty. I waited for about ten minutes past its scheduled meeting time and then returned to the departmental office. I told one of the secretaries that there must be some mistake: nobody was at the classroom. The secretary laughed and told me to be patient. They would eventually be there, usually about a half hour late. I returned to the classroom.

Sure enough, the class gradually appeared and was largely all there by a half hour after the scheduled time. I said nothing but at the second meeting of the class I began to lecture at the scheduled time, although no one was in the room. The first student arrived about ten minutes later. Standing in the doorway he looked into the room and saw this "nut" up there lecturing to an empty room. He scratched his head and quietly took a seat. A second student appeared a short time later and went through the same act of surprise. He sat next to the first student to arrive. Whispering, they exchanged their reactions while the lecture continued.

Once again the class eventually was completed. There was a great deal of whispering that went on as students arrived and took their seats. Again, I said nothing about the lateness. The conversations about my behavior continued after the class was adjourned.

When I arrived on time for the third session, the classroom was filled. It continued to be so through all the subsequent sessions.

LESSON LEARNED:

Talking to an empty room can fill it more quickly than talking to a filled room can empty it.

Mexico: A Tip on Corruption

Corruption in Mexico is a fine art. If the ingenuity employed in working out ways to acquire income illegally were used in seeking ways to acquire income legally, Mexico could well be the most economically developed country in the world.

BANRURAL is a bank established by the federal government to provide farmers with small loans with which to buy such necessities as seed, fertilizer and insecticides. In reviewing the loan record of the Bank, a colleague and I found that a very high percentage of the loans were not paid back: a much higher percentage than any bank in the US could survive. Much to our surprise we found that most of the loans were made to farmers who received loans each year despite their failure to pay them back.

We selected a sample of these farmers and reviewed their behavior in detail. We found that they regularly received a larger loan than they had asked for. But the excess was paid back to the loan clerk who had approved their loan. In return they were absolved of the need to pay back the amount they received.

Lesson Learned:
It is sometimes necessary to give in order to receive.

Mexico: Where Rank Has its Privileges

In Mexico appointments are not only uncertain because of waiting time but also because of rank. If a person of rank 2 has an appointment with someone he considers to be of rank 4 and someone of rank 3 comes along unexpectedly and asks for a meeting at the appointed time, 2 will cancel the meeting with 4 to meet with 3. He may or may not let 3 know of the cancellation. Even worse, if the caller for an appointment is of a higher rank than 2, a cancellation is expected and if not put into effect, it is taken as insult to 1 by 2.

The day before my stint in Mexico finished I had an appointment with my secretary at her home for lunch. That morning I received a call from the rector saying he had just heard about my leaving on the next day and asking if I could have lunch with him that afternoon. I told him I was sorry but I had a previous appointment.

My secretary put out the word (she was very good at this) about my failure to cancel my lunch with her. I became a hero to those at the bottom of the ladder and known as an uncouth foreigner by those at the top. Fortunately, the rector (who was a friend) was visiting the University of Pennsylvania in the next month and I made an appointment with him for lunch in Philadelphia. Of course, word of this did not get around. It would have reduced the shock value of my failure to do the expected canceling.

Lesson Learned:
In Mexico a person is his/her rank, not what he/she is.

Ford: Passing the Buck

We were working on a project for Ford's insurance business when I was approached by a senior vice president and asked if I would be interested in giving a two-day course to upper management. He elaborated. He wanted to cover 200 vice presidents in 10 classes: first, four classes of 20 junior vice presidents, then three classes of 20 intermediate vice presidents, followed by two classes of senior vice presidents, and finally one for vice presidents from the Executive Office. It was agreed that the last half day of each session would be devoted to discussion of issues raised by members of the class.

At the end of the first class held for junior vice presidents I was told by one of the class members that I was addressing the wrong group. They would like very much to use the ideas that I was suggesting but they could not do so without the approval of their bosses. They asked if I would I have a chance to expose their bosses to the same material. I told them I would do so in the next series of three classes. In each of the first four classes a junior vice president confronted me with the same issue.

In the next set of three classes with the intermediate level vice presidents the same issue was raised in each but this time involving the approval of senior vice presidents. In the two sessions for senior vice presidents they raised the same issue saying they required the approval of the Executive Office before they could implement any of the ideas I had suggested.

View of the boss from below

At this point I was dying of curiosity as to what implementation issue would be raised at the final session. The CEO of Ford attended that session and said he was anxious to apply my suggestions but that he could not do so without the support of his subordinates. He asked if I would have an opportunity to present the material to them.

The CEO completed a perfect example of passing the buck among managers who did not want to take responsibility for a change. The result was organizational paralysis. No one was willing to take the initiative. Ford remained unchanged.

LESSON LEARNED:

Passing the buck is a reflex that is symptomatic of organizational paralysis.

GSK Research

I had a meeting with the Vice President in charge of research at GlaxoSmithKline. He complained about the failure of his subordinates to implement a plan he had prepared for his division and which, he claimed, they had accepted when he had presented it to them. I tried to tell him why this was the case and why he should not keep trying to have it adopted. I suggested he start over again, preparing the plan in a participatory way. I tried to tell him why he would not succeed, but he was not willing to discuss it and he terminated the meeting before I had a chance to explain how I came to know that he would not succeed.

A number of years earlier, before the revolution that had overthrown the Shah, I was working on a project in Iran redesigning the Ministry of Health. The project was a joint effort between my group at Wharton and Iran's Industrial Management Institute. This institute, headed by Jamshid Gharajedaghi, was the largest of its kind in Iran. On one of my visits there I was met by Jamshid at the airport when I arrived. On our way to his offices he told me that the Shah wanted to talk to me and that he had made an appointment for me to do so on the next day.

When I asked how the Shah even knew of my existence, it turned out that Jamshid was the Scientific Adviser to the Queen. She had discussed with him a problem that bothered the Shah greatly. Jamshid had suggested the Shah meet with me because I had had some relevant experience with similar problems. The Shah was an absolute monarch; he could do much as he wanted to without being subject to correction. In fact, he was one the most powerful rulers in the world. Nevertheless the problem he wanted to discuss was this: Why couldn't he get any of his programs implemented as he wanted? His programs were either distorted in practice or stalled indefinitely. He was unable to find the cause of these implementation failures.

When Jamshid and I appeared at the palace the next day we were led to a plush waiting room and told that we would be called in a very few minutes. Shortly thereafter the man who had shown us to the waiting room came back to tell us the Shah had been called away suddenly on an emergency. We could hear and see his helicopter take off from the lawn of the palace. We were told, however, that the Queen would see us to discuss the problem the Shah had intended to talk about.

The Queen was a charming hostess who greeted us in a very large study filled with Louis XV furniture. A fire was blazing in a large fireplace that was flanked by two large sofas facing one another. The Queen took one and Jamshid and I were seated in the other. She presented the problem to us: the Shah's inability to have his programs implemented as he intended.

I believed I could explain this. The Shah had sent about forty thousand young Iranians to universities in Europe and the United States to pursue higher degrees. On completion of their degrees most had returned to Iran. Iran's business community was not advanced enough to absorb all this learning. The Shah believed that if these returnees were left unemployed they would become a dangerous political threat to him. So he had employed them in the government. As a result, Iran had one of the most highly educated governments in the world.

They did not agree with many of the programs the Shah tried to implement. Using their skills they were able to subvert these programs without the Shah being able to determine the cause of failure.

I suggested that the Shah create a constitutional monarchy much as England had, and that he appoint himself to the Supreme

Court, not as prime minister. The Queen said the Shah would not accept such a suggestion which, nevertheless, she would transmit to him. She said he believed it was only his absolute power that prevented the communists from taking over the government.

He reacted to the suggestion when it was transmitted to him exactly as the Queen had said he would. Nevertheless the revolution came shortly thereafter and it was led by the communists in collaboration with the religious right. It was the latter that gained control and annihilated the communists once their victory was assured.

LESSON LEARNED:
The more highly educated subordinates are, the less likely it is that the exercise of authority *(power over)* will be effective. The *power* to get them to do what their superior wants requires persuasion not dictation.

GE: Consumer Rationality

In the last quarter of the last century we were doing work at
GE's Appliance Park in Louisville, Kentucky. During a luncheon
at which we were informally discussing users of the division's
products, one of the managers remarked on how irrational
consumers were. I suggested it was better to assume that the
producer, not the customer, was irrational because if one assumed
the consumer was irrational, not much could be done about it.
But if the company was assumed to be irrational there was usually
a way to make it more effective.

This point of view was challenged. A particular example was
used. GE had conducted a national survey to find out which task
housewives found most onerous. The survey clearly revealed that
dish washing was the most disliked. This led GE to develop a
dish washing machine. It had been introduced to the market with
gusto. Nevertheless, it fell flat. Sales were very disappointing.

I suggested that a simple test be conducted. Appliance Park has a
large and impressive showroom. I suggested that one each of their
unsuccessful appliances be placed on one side of the room and
one each of their successful appliances be placed on the other side.
Then when this was completed we would enter and the reason for
failure might conceivably "hit us in the face". We actually placed
bets on the outcome.

A while later I received a call from Louisville telling me the time
for the test had arrived. I flew down the next day. To my surprise,
a chauffeur-driven limousine awaited me at the airport. There
was a red carpet running up the steps leading to the building
housing the show room. A trumpeter blew a call to assemble when
I arrived. There was a red ribbon stretched across the door to the

showroom. When we reached the door the ribbon was cut and we entered.

Not a word was spoken while we examined the displays. After no more than a few minutes the bets were settled in my favor. Every one of the unsuccessful appliances required the user to bend, stoop or climb. None of the successful appliances did; they were all in the "strike zone".

The original dishwasher, for example, had fixed drawers that required bending in order to load them. Before leaving the show room that morning the order went out to the engineers to make the drawers slide out so they could be loaded from above. This was done. The dishwasher became a very successful appliance.

LESSON LEARNED:
To attribute irrationality to another is to reveal one's own.

Clark Equipment: Leading and Following

James (Jim) Rinehart – appointed CEO of Clark Equipment in the 1980s – was one of the smartest people I have ever dealt with. His intelligence and learning were amazing. Although he made no effort to impress others with his superiority, those who came in contact with him were very aware of it.

I had convinced Jim to create an internal board consisting of all those executives who reported directly to him. The responsibilities of the board were planning, policy making, coordinating and integrating plans and policies made below it, making quality of working life decisions for the members of the board, and suggesting to Jim how he could make their jobs easier and more productive.

Jim asked me to run the first meeting of his board. It was held at the Kellogg Center of Notre Dame University which was close to Clark's headquarters in Buchanan, Michigan. Because all those present were aware of Jim's superior capabilities they waited on each issue to hear what he had to say about it. In some cases subsequent discussion amplified his suggestion but never contradicted it.

After several issues had been raised and had evoked the same response pattern I asked Jim to withhold his opinion until others had offered theirs. He agreed. However, when the next issue was raised it was followed by silence until Jim could no longer hold back and gave his opinion. I told Jim he would have to leave the room so that the other members of the board could participate more meaningfully. Reluctantly, Jim did so.

The meeting then brought forth widespread participation and a variety of positions to be considered. After about a half hour, Jim opened the door to the meeting room and asked if he could come back. I said he could if he sat in a corner and did not say anything. He did so. After about another half hour he asked if he could come back to the table. I told him he could, provided that he said nothing. He did so. Finally, after another period of time he asked if he could speak. I told him he could but only after the other members had had a chance to speak. He did so. Then, after a while, I asked him to take over the chair.

He did so and made an exemplary chairman of a very productive and provocative group. He later thanked me for what I had done to him. I doubt I could have gotten away with it had I not been older than Jim, a good friend with a great deal of relevant experience, and had he been someone of less intelligence.

LESSON LEARNED:

"Obsequious" literally means "following after". It is the willingness of others to follow after them that has empowered rulers, leaders and empires throughout history and been their Achilles' heel.

Clark Equipment: A Heroic Retreat

Clark, like many other manufacturers of mobile construction and material-handling equipment, suffered greatly when Komatsu, a large Japanese company, invaded the US market with superior equipment offered at a lower price. All but one division of the company was operating at a loss.

Jim Rinehart, the CEO, developed a plan for the company to divest itself of the losing divisions and retain the profitable one – rebuilding the business on its back. Clark's president, Leo McKernan, disagreed. He prepared a plan to make the losing divisions profitable again. The two men could not work out their difference. In the end, Jim Rinehart suggested they present the two strategies to the corporate board and have it make the choice. Then whoever was the author of the "losing" strategy would resign.

This was done and the Board chose McKernan's plan. Rinehart resigned with a very attractive package and went on to do development work for Hiram College, which was located near his home.

McKernan's plan did not succeed.

Lesson Learned:
It is better to start over than to end under.

Penn Tenure: On Giving Up Holding On

I have always been opposed to tenure attached to a university appointment. However, when I was appointed to a professorship at the University of Pennsylvania, tenure came along with it. Because I objected to it in principle I gave the relevant dean an undated letter of resignation that he could use whenever he wanted to get rid of me.

He's got tenure

I subsequently published my opposition to tenure, arguing that it protected incompetence more effectively than it protected academic freedom. Moreover there were more effective ways of protecting academic freedom which I supported enthusiastically. I was attacked by the local chapter of the American Association of University Professors (AAUP). It accused me of ignorance, not knowing the relevant facts.

I responded by proposing that we hire a research organization acceptable to both the AAUP and me and have it conduct a study to determine whether or not tenure protected incompetence more than it protected academic freedom. I suggested that the "losing" party foot the bill. The AAUP refused to take up the offer.

LESSON LEARNED:
Security über alles.

Kodak – Hotel

When working at Kodak in Rochester I was put up in a very nice small hotel in a residential section of the city. One day when I returned from work and went to the hotel, at which I had checked in the previous day, I went to my room to find a middle-aged woman sleeping in my bed. She woke when I entered the room and demanded an explanation. I told her she was in my room and it was me that wanted an explanation. She said I must be in the wrong room. I opened the closet and showed her my clothes. She then admitted that a mistake had been made.

She was to join her husband at the hotel. When she had arrived she was given my room number and key. We called the desk and said a mistake had obviously been made. After a short hunt the desk admitted to an error. The woman's husband was in a room across the hall. I left the room to stand in the hall while the lady dressed and gathered her belongings. While I was waiting, a bellhop, with a key to the correct room, appeared to assist us in moving her belongings.

When the lady appeared and her things had been collected, we went across the hall and started to open the door to her room; whereupon an angry man appeared from within and demanded an explanation from his wife for her lateness. Before she could answer I said she had arrived earlier and that I had found her in my bed. He looked as though he were ready to attack me when she and the bellhop hastened to explain the mistake made by the desk.

She was forgiven and given access to her husband's room and the door was closed leaving me to return to my room. A significantly revised version of this incident was circulated around Kodak, one that made me blush every time it was repeated.

Lesson Learned:
It is not right to say the right thing at the wrong time.

Rockwell: The Class

I was invited to "do a day" at an executive development course conducted for the Rockwell Corporation. It was held on the top floor of the William Penn Hotel in Pittsburgh. That floor had been converted into a training center by US Steel. It conducted its educational programs there and rented it to other companies when it was not in use.

At the end of my session in mid afternoon I left the room and entered the hall where I met the director of US Steel's programs. I knew him well because I had long been on the faculty of one of his programs. He asked me how the Rockwell session had gone. I told him it was the worst class I had ever addressed; its members were inert.

I did not know I still was wearing a wireless neck microphone that was still on. My remarks were received loud and clear back in the classroom.

I was not invited back.

Lesson Learned:
Unconsciously intended consequences can follow saying the right thing at the wrong time.

Union Institute: Sexism

After I left the Wharton School regular faculty, one of my students who had not completed his PhD brought the Union Institute in Cincinnati to my attention. It offered a non-residential PhD to mid career personnel in a very innovative way. I looked into the quality of the education it provided and found it to be quite high. I then arranged to join its faculty in order to take care of my "half baked" student. I was subsequently invited to address its annual faculty meeting held in Cincinnati.

In the course of my presentation I used the quotation, "So God created man in his own image". I was jumped on immediately by the female members of the faculty for being a sexist. I pointed out that his was a quotation from the bible. It had no effect. I also pointed out that "man" also meant "people in general". This too had no effect. They refused to go into any other aspect of my presentation. I left and resigned from that faculty.

The program was subsequently diluted by the state educational authority almost beyond recognition.

Lesson Learned:
Sexism is found in behavior not in language.

University Exits

I have left universities four times, each under rather unusual circumstances.

I graduated from the University of Pennsylvania School of Architecture in 1941. Shortly thereafter I was appointed to an assistantship in the Philosophy Department in which I had taken some elective courses as an undergraduate. Before my first semester as an assistant was over, Pearl Harbor occurred and I was drafted into the army early in January 1942. I was separated from the Army about four years later in 1946 after service in the Pacific theater. I resumed my teaching and studies in the fall of that year. This was a period of intense collaboration with my thesis supervisor, Professor C. West Churchman. (We were to collaborate for the next ten years, jointly producing several books and a number of articles.)

Churchman and I designed an Institute of Experimental Method that was intended to conduct interdisciplinary research and problem solving where societies were involved. We took our proposal to the President of the University who showed interest in it. He said he would create such an Institute if we could get the support in writing of three different departments. It took almost a year to get the approvals required. In the meantime the President had retired due to illness and had been replaced by a lower level officer of the University. When we showed him the proposal and conditions for approval that his predecessor had established, he told us he was not bound by agreements made by his predecessor. He showed no interest in our proposal. I took this as a rejection of our idea and saw no reason to remain at Penn even if I could have.

I graduated with a PhD in the spring of 1947. During the summer that followed I accepted an appointment in the Philosophy

Department of Wayne University in Detroit. (It was not then a state supported institution. That came later, after I had left the University.) The Dean of the College had assured me that he would support the creation of an Institute much like the one Penn had rejected. It was to be called the Institute of Applied Philosophy.

The Philosophy Department, which I joined as an Assistant Professor, consisted of two professors. They were not happy with my efforts to apply philosophy. They considered it to be prostitution of the field. In particular in my second year in that department I put on a conference on the application of philosophy to city planning. This was done with the collaboration of Detroit's Director of City Planning. The chairman of the Philosophy Department had tried to dissuade me from promoting and participating in such a venture. When I did not take his advice, he did not renew my annual contract for a third year. In addition, it became apparent at this time that the Dean would not support the creation of our Institute because of opposition from the Philosophy Department. Fortunately, the Mathematics Department picked up my appointment and I joined it.

The Mathematics Department was very supportive but it became obvious that I was occupying a faculty position that was intended for a much needed mathematical theoretician. I felt that I was an obstruction to a Department that had been more than kind to me. I resigned from the Department in 1951 to open up that position. I planned to return to architecture when deep into the summer an opportunity arose for Churchman (who had joined me at Wayne) and me to join the faculty at Case Institute of Technology in Cleveland, Ohio.

Keith Glennan, the very supportive President of Case, together with Clay Hollister, the equally supportive Chairman of the Engineering Administration Department, enabled us to create an academic and research program in Operations Research. Our program thrived over the next 13 years. Clay Hollister left in the early 1960s, but his successor, Vern Michaelson was equally supportive.

Unfortunately, Keith Glennan became ill in 1963 and announced his resignation to take place at the end of the next academic year. Case's board then conducted a search for a new president. They selected John Hrones who was then a professor at MIT. He joined Case for the academic year 1963-64 while Glennan was still there. Hrones, acting as president, installed some procedures that I found intolerable. He placed a quota on foreign students of which we had many. He also required his approval for the appointment of any graduate students to a research or teaching post within the department. Since he had no knowledge of our field I felt this was nothing but a bureaucratic hurdle that would do nothing for the quality of the students we were appointing.

I spoke to Glennan about these and other disagreements with Hrones. He asked me to be patient and give him time to try to "straighten things out". It was agreed that if nothing were done about these issues I would resign in February of 1964. Despite his efforts and mine the issues were not resolved by then. I submitted my resignation from Case to take effect at the end of the 1964 spring semester.

In another one of these memories ('From Case to Penn') I describe how we came to go to The Wharton School of the University of Pennsylvania in September 1964. There too it was a problem with an administrator, a dean, that led to my resignation two years before I reached the age at which retirement was compulsory at that time.

LESSON LEARNED:

It is much easier to leave an institution than to enter it. And the institution is much more grateful for it.

Also Available from Triarchy Press

By the same author:

Management f-Laws ~ Russell Ackoff (with Herbert Addison and Sally Bibb)

In the same vein as Sod's Law and Parkinson's Law, here are 80 of Russ Ackoff's subversive insights into the world of business and organizations, with ripostes from Sally Bibb.

Systems Thinking for Curious Managers ~ Russell Ackoff (with Herbert Addison and Andrew Carey)

An introduction to Systems Thinking and Russ Ackoff's view of organizations, including 40 more, previously unpublished, management f-laws.

Differences that Make a Difference ~ Russell Ackoff

A witty and wicked "Glossary of Distinctions Important in Management", introducing Ackoff's notion of ecological systems.

On Systems and Design Thinking:

The Innovation Acid Test: Growth Through Design and Differentiation ~ Andrew Jones

How Design Thinking underpins the world's most dynamic, successful companies, and how to apply it any organization.

Systems Thinking in the Public Sector ~ John Seddon

A devastating critique of targets, incentives, inspection, economies of scale, shared back-office services and 'deliverology' in public services.

The Search for Leadership: An Organisational Perspective ~ William Tate

Explains why conventional leadership models miss the point and presents a Systems Thinking approach that focuses on the organization rather than individual leaders.

Delivering Public Services that Work ~ Peter Middleton with John Seddon

A ground-breaking collection of Case Studies showing how Systems Thinking has been applied to a particular public service in six local authorities.

Economies of Life: Patterns of Health and Wealth ~ Bill Sharpe

Argues that there are many economies, (not just the one based on money), and that they all contribute to the health and sustainability of our shared lives. In this model, money is the currency of trade and art is the currency of experience.

About Triarchy Press

Triarchy Press is an independent publishing house that looks at how organisations work and how to make them work better. We present challenging perspectives on organisations in short and pithy, but rigorously argued, books.

Through our books, pamphlets and website we aim to stimulate ideas by encouraging real debate about organisations in partnership with people who work in them, research them or just like to think about them.

Please tell us what you think about the ideas in this book at:

www.triarchypress.com/telluswhatyouthink

If you feel inspired to write – or have already written – an article, a pamphlet or a book on any aspect of organisational theory or practice, we'd like to hear from you. Submit a proposal at:

www.triarchypress.com/writeforus

For more information about Triarchy Press, or to order any of our publications, please visit our website or drop us a line:

www.triarchypress.com

We're now on Twitter:

@TriarchyPress

and Facebook:

www.facebook.com/triarchypress

Breinigsville, PA USA
21 October 2010
247779BV00004B/12/P

9 780956 537973